Fire Up the Grill!

Woman's Day

Fire Up the Grill!

Over 75 recipes for great dining outdoors

filipacchi
publishing

Filipacchi Publishing
1633 Broadway
New York, NY 10019

© 2003 Filipacchi Publishing

Designed by Patricia Fabricant
Copyedited by Margaret Farley, Greg Robertson and
Kim Walker

ISBN 2-85018-653-8

Printed and bound in Italy

Contents

Fire Up the Grill!

What could be more all-American than backyard grilling? We all have memories of summer days when the sizzle and smell of the barbecue were a call that dinner was ready. Back then, cooking on the grill usually meant burgers, franks, steaks, ribs and the occasional chicken breast. But times have changed.

With *Fire Up the Grill!*, *Woman's Day* has fast-forwarded grilling into the 21st century. Readers have always turned to *Woman's Day* for nutritious, easy and timesaving recipes. Now we help you think in a completely new way about traditional grilling. Yes, there are burgers and chicken dishes. There are also recipes that go far beyond the same-old, same-old. Have you ever considered grilled lamb, pork, seafood or veggies? Take your pick of tantalizing international dishes from the Caribbean to the Mediterranean to the Pacific Rim. And, of course, there's lots of down-home American flavor, from finger-lickin' Barbecue Ribs to Grilled Chicken Pizza. These are dishes that are sure to please, whether you're trying to stimulate the palate of a finicky child or surprise a sophisticated adult. We show you how to do them, no mess, no fuss. Sandwiches, exotic salads, exciting entrees, even a grilled fruit dessert—you name it, it's here, along with the tips and tricks that make prep and cooking fast and easy. We also include the sides and add-ons you need to create a full meal, including dips, salsas, drinks and desserts.

Fire Up the Grill! offers something for everyone and every occasion, from the simplest backyard family barbecue to an elaborate alfresco dinner party under the stars. The possibilities are so endless, you may never go back to the kitchen.

Chicken with Walnut-Basil Crust

CRUST
  1 cup loosely packed basil leaves
  3/4 cup walnut pieces
  1/4 cup grated Parmesan cheese
  3 large cloves garlic
  1/4 tsp each salt and pepper
1 broiler-fryer chicken (3 1/2 lb), quartered and skin removed

1 Process Crust ingredients in food processor to a fine paste. Pat over top and sides of chicken pieces.

2 To grill with charcoal using indirect heat: Build a fire with about 20 briquettes on 1 side of grill. Set grill 4 to 6 in. above coals. When coals are medium-hot (400°F), arrange chicken, crust side up, on side of grill without briquettes.

3 Cover grill and cook 30 to 40 minutes until chicken is opaque near the bone. For gas grills: Follow manufacturer's instructions for indirect grilling.

PREP: 20 min
GRILL: 30 to 40 min

SERVES 4

PER SERVING: 450 cal, 47 g pro, 6 g car, 2 g fiber, 26 g fat (5 g saturated fat), 130 mg chol, 362 mg sod

GRILLING TIPS

- FOR GAS GRILLS: Preheat grill on high 10 minutes (or until 500°F to 550°F), then adjust heat and follow manufacturer's directions.

- FOR CHARCOAL GRILLS: Start the fire 30 minutes before grilling and let the coals burn until covered with a gray-white ash before cooking.

PREP: 10 min
GRILL: 9 to 11 min

SERVES 4

PER SERVING: 411 cal,
  35 g pro, 36 g car, 2 g fiber,
  14 g fat (5 g saturated fat),
  70 mg chol, 1,151 mg sod

Grilled Chicken Pizza

3 skinless, boneless chicken breast halves (about 12 oz)
3/4 cup bottled balsamic vinaigrette
1 tube (10 oz) pizza crust
Garlic-flavor nonstick spray
1 cup shredded part-skim mozzarella cheese
1/4 cup grated Parmesan cheese
1 cup diced plum (Roma) tomatoes
1 cup lightly packed torn arugula or basil leaves

1 Heat barbecue grill. While grill heats, place chicken and vinaigrette in a ziptop bag and seal; turn to coat.

2 Line a baking sheet with foil; coat foil with nonstick spray. Unroll pizza dough on sheet; press into a 12 x 9-in. rectangle. Coat dough with nonstick spray.

3 Remove chicken from bag and grill, turning once, 7 to 8 minutes, until lightly charred and cooked through. Remove to a cutting board. Cut crosswise in 1/2-in.-thick slices.

4 Invert pizza dough onto grill; peel off foil. Grill 1 minute or until the underside is lightly browned. Turn crust over and grill 30 seconds or until underside stiffens. Scatter top with 3/4 cup mozzarella cheese, then the chicken, remaining mozzarella cheese and the Parmesan cheese.

5 Cover and grill 1 to 2 minutes until cheese melts, making sure underside of pizza doesn't burn.

6 Transfer to a cutting board; top with tomato and arugula, then cut in 4 pieces.

Grilled Chicken Sandwich with Avocado, Corn and Tomato Salsa

SALSA
- *1/4 cup fresh lime juice*
- *2 Tbsp canola oil*
- *2 tsp sugar*
- *1/2 tsp salt*
- *1 ripe avocado, peeled, seeded and diced*
- *1 large ripe tomato, diced*
- *1 cup thawed frozen or drained canned corn kernels*
- *1/4 cup chopped red onion*
- *1/4 cup chopped fresh cilantro or parsley*
- *4 skinless, boneless chicken breast halves (about 4 oz each)*
- *1/4 tsp each salt and pepper*
- *1 tsp dried oregano*
- *4 crusty rolls*
- *1 1/2 cups shredded lettuce*
- *8 slices tomato*

1 Mix lime juice, oil, sugar and salt for Salsa in a medium bowl. Add avocado, tomato, corn, onion and cilantro and toss gently to mix.

2 Heat barbecue grill. Season chicken with salt, pepper and oregano. Grill chicken 3 to 4 minutes per side until cooked through.

3 Cut rolls in half. Top bottom half of each with shredded lettuce, tomato, 1 chicken breast and 1/2 cup Salsa. Replace tops of rolls. Serve remaining Salsa on the side.

PREP:	30 min
GRILL:	6 to 8 min

SERVES 4

PER SERVING: 507 cal, 35 g pro, 51 g car, 4 g fiber, 19 g fat (2 g saturated), 66 mg chol, 833 mg sod

GRILLING TIPS

- *Before heating, use a grill brush to clean off any food left from the grill's last use.*

- *Never partially grill meat or poultry and completely finish cooking it later.*

- *Before grilling, brush oil on the grill to prevent sticking and to get great grill marks.*

SERVES 4

PER SERVING: 271 cal,
 34 g pro, 2 g car, 0 g fiber,
 13 g fat (2 g saturated fat),
 85 mg chol, 378 mg sod

GRILLED TOMATO & CHICKPEA SALAD

Mix **1/3 cup bottled Italian dressing** and **1 1/2 tsp minced garlic** in a medium bowl. Add **1 can (19 oz) rinsed chickpeas** and **1/3 cup basil leaves**, loosely packed, stacked and cut in narrow strips; toss to mix. Cut **2 large, firm, ripe tomatoes** in half crosswise, and lightly coat with **nonstick spray**. Grill, turning tomatoes over once, 3 minutes or until slightly charred. Top with chickpea mixture; serve tomatoes hot or at room temperature.

SERVES 4

PER SERVING: 197 cal,
 6 g pro, 20 g car, 6 g fiber,
 11 g fat (1 g saturated fat),
 0 mg chol, 358 mg sod

Herb and Mustard Chicken

MARINADE
 1/4 cup purchased basil pesto
 3 Tbsp bottled balsamic vinaigrette
 1 Tbsp spicy brown mustard
4 skinless, boneless chicken breast halves (about 5 oz each)

1 Mix Marinade ingredients in a large ziptop bag. Add chicken; press air from bag, seal and turn to coat. Refrigerate at least 30 minutes or up to 1 hour.

2 Heat barbecue grill. Remove chicken from Marinade; discard Marinade.

3 Grill chicken 4 minutes per side or until cooked through. Transfer to a cutting board; let rest 5 minutes.

4 Cut each breast crosswise in 1-in.-wide slices.

WHAT'S HOT?

Unless your charcoal grill has a thermometer, the best way to judge the heat of the coals is to very carefully hold your hand above them.

	TEMPERATURE	CONDITION OF COALS	SECONDS YOU CAN HOLD HAND OVER COALS (AT COOKING HEIGHT)
SEARING	450°F–500°F (very hot)	glowing with some gray ashes around edges	1 to 2
GRILLING	400°F–500°F (hot)	gray ash covers coals	2 to 3
COVERED COOKING	350°F–400°F	coals halfway to ashes	4 to 5

PREP:	20 min
GRILL:	5 to 6 min

SERVES 4

PER SERVING: 414 cal,
36 g pro, 17 g car, 3 g fiber,
24 g fat (3 g saturated fat),
82 mg chol, 325 mg sod

Jamaican Jerk Chicken Salad

2 tsp Jamaican Jerk Rub (see There's the Rub, right)
4 skinless, boneless chicken breast halves (about 5 oz each)
Nonstick cooking spray

DRESSING
   1/4 cup olive oil
   1/4 cup orange juice
   1 tsp cider vinegar
   1/4 tsp each salt and ground red pepper (cayenne)
8 oz green-leaf or other lettuce torn in bite-size pieces
   (8 cups, loosely packed)
1 firm ripe mango, peeled, cut in bite-size pieces
1 medium-size cucumber, cut in bite-size chunks (1 1/2 cups)
1/3 cup thinly sliced red onion
1/3 cup coarsely chopped toasted hazelnuts (see Tip)

1 Sprinkle 1/4 tsp Jerk Rub over 1 side of each breast half, then spread over surface with fingers. Repeat with other side of breast. Lightly coat both sides with cooking spray.

2 Grill 4 to 6 in. above hot coals 5 to 6 minutes, turning once, until opaque in middle.

3 Meanwhile whisk Dressing ingredients in a large serving bowl until well blended.

4 Cut chicken in half lengthwise, then crosswise in bite-size pieces. Add lettuce, remaining ingredients and the chicken to bowl. Toss, coat with Dressing and mix.

TIP To toast hazelnuts: Heat oven to 350°F. Spread nuts in a baking pan. Bake 8 to 10 minutes until toasted and skins begin to flake. Turn out onto a towel and rub off papery skins.

The hot new trend in barbecuing these days is rubs, and for good reason. These dry marinades cling to food and help meats brown better than they do with a wet marinade. Combine the herbs and spices in any of these seasoning mixtures, then rub them all over meats and poultry.

JAMAICAN JERK 4 tsp ground allspice, 1 Tbsp each dried thyme and paprika, 1 tsp each ground red pepper (cayenne), garlic powder, onion powder and salt and 1/4 tsp black pepper

MEXICAN 2 Tbsp hot Mexican chili powder, 1 tsp each ground cumin, dried oregano, garlic powder and salt and 1/4 tsp ground cloves

TANDOORI 1 1/2 tsp each garlic powder and paprika, 1 tsp each ground red pepper (cayenne), ground coriander, ground cumin, ground ginger and salt and 1/4 tsp each ground cardamom and ground cinnamon

PREP: 10 min
GRILL: 40 to 45 min

SERVES 4

PER SERVING: 424 cal,
32 g pro, 52 g car, 6 g fiber,
9 g fat (4 g saturated fat),
115 mg chol, 493 mg sod

TIP *To cook potatoes in microwave: Arrange 1 in. apart on paper towels in microwave. Cook on high 12 to 16 minutes, turning potatoes over after 6 minutes, until soft. Let stand 3 minutes. To bake: Bake in 425°F oven about 45 minutes until soft. Proceed with potatoes in Step 4.*

Tandoori Chicken with Sweet Potatoes

4 chicken legs (2 lb), thighs and drumsticks separated, skin removed
4 medium sweet potatoes (about 8 oz each), scrubbed

MARINADE
  1 cup plain lowfat yogurt
  1 Tbsp curry powder
  1 1/2 tsp minced fresh ginger
  1 tsp minced garlic
  1 tsp paprika
  1/2 tsp salt
1/4 cup golden raisins
1 Tbsp butter
GARNISH: *chopped cilantro or parsley*

1 With a small pointed knife, cut 1-in.-deep slits about 1 in. apart in chicken. Pierce potatoes and wrap bottom halves with foil (see Tip if not grilling).

2 Heat grill. Mix Marinade ingredients in a large bowl. Add chicken; turn to coat, rubbing some marinade into slits.

3 Place potatoes near edges of grill, away from direct heat to prevent scorching. Cover grill and cook potatoes 10 minutes. Add chicken to grill (reserve Marinade in bowl), cover grill and cook 30 to 35 minutes, turning chicken once and basting with reserved Marinade after 15 minutes, until juices run clear when meat is pierced and potatoes are soft.

4 Cut a slit in top of potatoes; push ends toward center to open. Add raisins and butter, then sprinkle with cilantro.

Citrus Chicken with Cilantro

MARINADE
- *1 cup fresh orange juice*
- *1/2 cup fresh lime juice*
- *1 Tbsp ground cumin*
- *1 1/2 tsp salt*
- *1 tsp pepper*
- *10 cloves garlic, smashed*
- *2 chickens (3 1/2 lb each), cut in eighths, excess fat trimmed (see Tip)*
- *1 cup loosely packed cilantro, chopped*
- *GARNISH: orange wedges*

1 Divide Marinade ingredients between 2 large, sturdy ziptop bags. Add 1 cut-up chicken to each. Press air from bags, seal and turn bags over a few times to mix ingredients and coat chickens. Refrigerate at least 3 hours or overnight.

2 Heat barbecue grill. Grill chicken 4 to 6 in. above heat source 40 minutes or until heated through, turning pieces over occasionally to prevent burning.

3 Place on serving platter. Sprinkle with the cilantro and garnish with the orange wedges.

PREP: 15 min
MARINATE: 3 hr to overnight
GRILL: About 40 min

SERVES 8

PER SERVING: 432 cal, 48 g pro, 3 g car, 0 g fiber, 24 g fat (7 g saturated fat), 154 mg chol, 364 mg sod

TIP *Use kitchen scissors to snip all visible fat off chicken.*

PLANNING TIP *The chicken can be marinated in ziptop bags and the cilantro chopped up to 1 day ahead. Refrigerate separately.*

PREP: 6 min
COOK: 2 min
GRILL: 8 to 12 min

SERVES 4

PER SERVING: 286 cal,
37 g pro, 5 g car, 1 g fiber,
13 g fat (3 g saturated fat),
82 mg chol, 468 mg sod

SAFE GRILLING

- Don't use a grill when it's very windy.

- Position grill in an open area away from buildings and trees.

- To extinguish coals, close all vents and cover the grill with a lid. Check coals several hours later to make sure they are extinguished.

Chicken with Peanut Saté Sauce

SATE SAUCE
  1/4 cup peanut butter
  2 Tbsp reduced-sodium soy sauce
  2 Tbsp each fresh lime juice and water
  1 tsp each minced fresh ginger and garlic
  1/2 tsp dark Oriental sesame oil
  1/8 tsp ground red pepper (cayenne)
2 tsp vegetable oil
4 skinless, boneless chicken breast halves (about 5 oz each)
1 scallion, sliced
GARNISH: grilled whole scallions

1 Whisk Saté Sauce ingredients in a small saucepan until blended. Spoon off 2 Tbsp and reserve.

2 Heat grill.

3 Brush oil on both sides of chicken breasts. Place 4 to 6 in. from heat source. Grill 4 minutes, turning chicken over once. Brush both sides with reserved Sauce and cook, turning once, 4 to 6 minutes until chicken is opaque in center.

4 Meanwhile stir scallion into remaining Sauce. Heat over low heat, stirring occasionally. Serve with chicken; garnish plates with grilled scallions.

Rosemary-Scented Chicken

1/4 cup chopped fresh rosemary
2 large cloves garlic
1 tsp each salt and freshly ground pepper
2 Tbsp extra-virgin olive oil
4 skinless, boneless chicken breast halves (about 5 oz each)
2 Tbsp very good quality balsamic vinegar

1 Heat grill to high and brush with oil. Mash rosemary, garlic, salt and pepper in a mortar with a pestle, then stir in the oil. (Or finely chop the garlic, rosemary and salt with a large knife. Put into a small bowl; stir in pepper and oil.) Spread evenly over both sides of chicken.

2 Grill 3 to 5 minutes per side or until just cooked through (see Tip). Transfer to a serving platter and drizzle evenly with vinegar. Serve hot or at room temperature.

PREP: 7 min
GRILL: 6 to 10 min

SERVES 4

PER SERVING: 223 cal,
33 g pro, 2 g car, 0 g fiber,
9 g fat (2 g saturated fat),
82 mg chol, 676 mg sod

NOTE Sometimes simple preparation is best, especially on the grill. Fresh rosemary and tangy balsamic vinegar make this chicken the delight that it is. Only fresh rosemary will do. Dried rosemary simply isn't right for this dish.

TIP To get restaurant-style crosshatch markings on the chicken breasts, give them a quarter-turn halfway through grilling on each side.

Mixed Grill with Polenta

1 Tbsp balsamic vinegar
1 small clove garlic
4 red and 2 yellow bell peppers, halved and seeded
2 large (12 oz) portobello mushrooms, stems removed
2 medium red onions, sliced 1/2 in. thick
1 roll (24 oz) heat-and-serve polenta with basil and garlic,
  cut in 1/2-in.-thick rounds (see Tip)
Olive oil nonstick cooking spray
4 precooked chicken and turkey sausages with sundried
  tomatoes and Parmesan cheese

1 Put vinegar and garlic in blender or food processor.

2 Heat barbecue grill.

3 Grill peppers, mushrooms and onions, turning as needed, until slightly charred and tender: peppers 12 to 15 minutes, mushrooms and onions 6 to 8 minutes. Remove vegetables to cutting board.

4 Lightly coat polenta slices with cooking spray. Grill polenta and sausages about 4 minutes, turning as needed until slightly charred and hot. Place on serving platter.

5 Add 4 of the red bell-pepper halves to ingredients in the blender or food processor. Purée until smooth. Cut remaining peppers in 1-in. strips and mushrooms in 1/2-in. slices. Add vegetables to platter; serve with red-pepper sauce.

PREP: 8 min
GRILL: 16 to 19 min

SERVES 4

PER SERVING: 375 cal, 20 g pro, 49 g car, 7 g fiber, 11 g fat (3 g saturated), 10 mg chol, 773 mg sod

TIP *No need to make labor-intensive polenta, a delicious Italian side dish, from scratch. You can now buy cylinders of precooked, fat-free plain or flavored polenta in many supermarkets, often in the produce section.*

GRILLING TIP

Don't crowd the grill. Too much food too close together hampers air flow, slows cooking and steams the food, which keeps it from browning.

PREP: 15 min
GRILL: 10 to 12 min

SERVES 4

PER SERVING: 533 cal,
32 g pro, 56 g car, 5 g fiber,
21 g fat (7 g saturated fat),
127 mg chol, 759 mg sod

THREE-ONION RELISH

Cook **1 1/2 cups chopped yellow onions** in **1 Tbsp vegetable oil** in a skillet over medium-low heat 5 to 8 minutes until golden and tender. Remove from heat and stir in **1/4 cup sliced scallions and 1/4 cup chopped red onion.** Cool relish and serve warm or at room temperature.

NO-COOK CORN RELISH

Mix **1 can (11 oz) whole-kernel corn**, drained, **1 can (8 3/4 oz) creamed corn, 1/4 cup** *each* **chopped celery and red bell pepper, 2 Tbsp cider vinegar, 2 tsp Dijon mustard,** and **1 tsp minced onion** in medium-size bowl. Serve at room temperature or cover and refrigerate up to one week.

Cantina Burgers with Corn on the Cob

4 ears corn
1 lb lean ground beef
2/3 cup crushed baked corn-taco chips
1/2 cup milk
1/3 cup sliced scallions
1 large egg
1 tsp ground cumin
1/2 tsp salt
4 kaiser rolls
ACCOMPANIMENTS: *green-leaf lettuce, sliced avocado and salsa for burgers; butter for corn*

1 Heat grill. Pull husks back from corn, remove silks, then smooth husks back in place. Soak corn in cold water about 10 minutes. Drain well.

2 Meanwhile mix beef, corn-taco chips, milk, sliced scallions, egg, cumin and salt just until blended. Shape into 4 patties, about 1 in. thick.

3 Place corn and burgers on grill. Grill corn, turning ears occasionally, 10 to 12 minutes until the husks are charred and the kernels are tender, and burgers 4 to 5 minutes per side for medium.

4 Serve burgers on rolls with green-leaf lettuce, sliced avocado and salsa, and corn with butter.

All-American Grilled Steak

CREAMY BLUE-CHEESE TOPPING
   1/2 cup (2 oz) crumbled blue cheese, at room temperature
   2 oz 1/3-less-fat cream cheese (Neufchâtel), softened
   1/4 cup snipped chives or minced scallion greens
2 tsp vegetable oil
3/4 tsp each hot-pepper sauce and salt
1 1/2 lb top round beef steak for London broil (about 1 in. thick)

1 Heat barbecue grill until hot.

2 Mix the Creamy Blue-Cheese Topping ingredients in a small bowl with a fork.

3 Mix oil, hot-pepper sauce and salt in another small bowl. Brush on both sides of the steak.

4 Grill, turning once, 12 to 14 minutes for medium-rare, 20 to 22 minutes for medium (see Tip).

5 Transfer to cutting board; let rest 5 minutes. Thinly slice across the grain. Serve with a dollop of Topping.

PREP: 10 min
GRILL: 12 to 22 min

SERVES 6

PER SERVING: 270 cal,
   26 g pro, 0 g car, 0 g fiber,
   18 g fat (8 g saturated fat),
   80 mg chol, 530 mg sod

TIP *Cooking the steak longer may make it tough.*

SOUTHERN SWEET-POTATO SALAD

Cook **2 lb sweet potatoes,** peeled and cut in 3/4-in. chunks, in water to cover 12 to 15 minutes until just tender. Drain. Submerge in ice water 3 minutes; drain well. Place in a serving bowl. Meanwhile cook **5 slices bacon** in a large nonstick skillet 8 minutes or until crisp. Drain on paper towels, then crumble. Pour bacon fat from skillet. Add **1/2 cup chopped pecans** and cook 1 to 2 minutes, stirring once or twice, until aromatic and toasted. Add pecans, **1 cup chopped celery, 1/2 cup chopped red onion and 1/2 cup bottled vinaigrette dressing** to potatoes. Toss gently to mix and coat. Sprinkle with bacon and **chopped celery leaves.**

PREP: 23 min

SERVES 6

PER SERVING: 253 cal,
   4 g pro, 32 g car, 4 g fiber,
   12 g fat (2 g saturated fat),
   4 mg chol, 304 mg sod

PREP: 10 min
GRILL: 35 to 47 min

SERVES 4

PER SERVING: 223 cal,
  25 g pro, 16 g car, 6 g fiber,
  7 g fat (2 g saturated fat),
  54 mg chol, 346 mg sod

FOR ADDED FLAVOR

Soak a small bundle of fresh basil, oregano, thyme or rosemary in cool water for about 30 minutes, then toss it on the coals during the last 30 minutes of grilling.

CHICKEN-BREAST POTATO-PACKET VARIATION

Prepare as directed in Steps 1 and 2, substituting **4 skinless, boneless chicken breast halves** (about 5 oz each) for the London broil; **4 medium all-purpose potatoes,** scrubbed, halved lengthwise and thinly sliced for the red-skinned potatoes; and **1 lb asparagus,** woody stems broken off, remaining spears cut in 2-in. pieces for the red bell pepper. Proceed as directed, adding chicken to grill after packets have cooked 20 minutes. Grill chicken 40 to 50 minutes per side until opaque in center.

Peppery London Broil with Potato Packets

SPICE RUB

  1 tsp each *paprika, dry mustard and chili powder*
  1/2 tsp each *garlic powder and coarsely ground black pepper*
  1/8 tsp *ground red pepper (cayenne)*
1 lb 1-in.-thick *boneless beef top round for London broil, fat trimmed*
1 1/2 lb *red-skinned potatoes (about 6 medium), scrubbed and thinly sliced*
1 *red bell pepper, halved, cored and cut in narrow strips*
1 medium *onion, thinly sliced*
1 Tbsp *olive oil*
1/2 tsp each *dried thyme and salt*

1 Mix Spice Rub ingredients in a small bowl. Have ready four 12-in.-long strips of heavy-duty foil.

2 Rub Spice Rub onto both sides of meat. Heat grill.

3 Mix remaining ingredients in a bowl. Divide mixture among the 4 pieces of foil, placing mixture near one end. Fold in half to form packet; fold edges to seal completely.

4 Grill packets 25 to 30 minutes, turning over once, until potatoes are tender when pierced. After packets have cooked 25 minutes (remove if done), add steak to grill. Grill 5 to 7 minutes per side for rare, 7 to 9 minutes for medium and 9 to 11 minutes for well done.

Steak Fajita Salad

2 tsp each *ground cumin and dried oregano*
1/2 tsp each *chili powder and garlic salt*
1 tsp *vegetable oil, preferably canola*
1 lb *1-in.-thick flank steak or boneless beef top round steak
  for London broil, fat trimmed*
1/2 cup *bottled light Catalina salad dressing*
1 head *romaine lettuce, washed and cut up*
2 cups each *shredded carrots and red cabbage (from 10-oz bags)*
1 can *(about 15 oz) black beans, rinsed*
1 can *(11 oz) golden whole-kernel corn, drained*
3 medium *tomatoes, each cut in 8 wedges*

1 Heat grill.

2 Mix 1 tsp *each* cumin and oregano, and the chili powder and garlic salt in a small bowl. Rub vegetable oil, then seasonings on both sides of meat.

3 Grill 5 to 7 minutes per side for rare, 7 to 9 minutes for medium and 9 to 11 minutes for well done. Remove to a cutting board, cover loosely with aluminum foil and let rest about 10 minutes before thinly slicing across the grain.

4 Meanwhile pour salad dressing into the small bowl and stir in remaining 1 tsp *each* cumin and oregano.

5 Place romaine, carrots, cabbage, black beans and corn in a large salad bowl. Add dressing; toss to mix and coat. Divide among 6 large serving plates or bowls, top with sliced steak and surround with tomato wedges.

PREP: 20 min
GRILL: 10 to 22 min

SERVES 6

PER SERVING: 300 cal,
  22 g pro, 30 g car, 7 g fiber,
  11 g fat (3 g saturated fat),
  38 mg chol, 655 mg sod

NOTE As an added topping, cut flavored or plain flour tortillas in strips and panfry in a little oil until crisp. Drain on paper towels and sprinkle on each salad.

GRILLING TIP

To speed heating time of charcoal, use a portable hair dryer. The hot air forced across the coals causes them to glow with a light flame that will spread instantly. (But keep plastic dryers well away from intense heat: they melt.)

PREP: 30 min
GRILL: 9 to 12 min

SERVES 4

PER SERVING: 510 cal,
  31 g pro, 44 g car, 4 g fiber,
  23 g fat (6 g saturated fat),
  68 mg chol, 981 mg sod

GRILLING TIP

To tell if your steak is done, touch the meat with your fingers and gently press. Then turn your arm so your thumb is facing up. Press down on your wrist, the middle of your forearm and the fleshy area at your elbow. If the meat feels like your wrist, it's well done. If it's like your forearm, it's medium, and if it feels like your soft elbow area, it's medium-rare.

Thai Beef Salad

PEANUT DRESSING
  1/3 cup bottled Oriental salad dressing
  1 Tbsp creamy peanut butter
About 12 large outer leaves green-leaf lettuce
1/4 of a long English seedless (hothouse) cucumber,
  cut lengthwise in quarters, then thinly sliced
1/2 cup fresh mint leaves
1/2 cup shredded carrots
1/4 cup unsalted dry roasted peanuts, coarsely chopped
One 1-lb, 1-in.-thick boneless sirloin steak
Nonstick spray
1/2 tsp each salt and freshly ground pepper
4 pocketless or regular pitas

1 Heat barbecue grill.

2 Whisk Peanut Dressing ingredients in a small bowl; scrape into a serving dish.

3 Place lettuce leaves and mounds of cucumber, mint, carrots and peanuts on a large serving platter. Refrigerate.

4 Coat both sides of steak with nonstick spray; season with salt and pepper. Grill, turning once, 8 to 10 minutes for medium-rare (140°F on a meat thermometer inserted in middle). Remove to a cutting board; let rest 5 minutes (meat will continue to cook).

5 Meanwhile grill pita 1 to 2 minutes, turning once, until lightly toasted.

6 Thinly slice steak across the grain; place on another serving platter with the pita. Let diners place steak slices in the middle of a lettuce leaf. Put out cucumber, mint, carrots, peanuts and Peanut Dressing for diners to top the steak. Roll up; eat out of hand. Serve with pitas.

Open-Face Italian Steak Sandwiches

PESTO MAYONNAISE
  1/2 cup basil pesto, purchased or homemade (see Tip)
  2 Tbsp light mayonnaise
One 1-lb, 1-in.-thick boneless sirloin steak
4 slices (about 3/4 in. thick) from a round loaf Italian
  or sourdough bread
Garlic-flavor nonstick cooking spray
1/2 tsp each salt and pepper
1 bunch arugula or watercress, leaves torn if large
  (about 4 cups)
1 large ripe tomato, cut in 8 slices

1 Heat barbecue grill. Mix the basil pesto and mayonnaise in a small bowl.

2 Spray both sides of steak and bread with garlic-flavor spray; season steak with salt and pepper.

3 Grill steak 4 to 6 in. above heat source 12 minutes, turning over once, for medium-rare. Remove to a cutting board and let rest 5 minutes.

4 Meanwhile grill bread 2 to 3 minutes, turning over once, until lightly toasted.

5 Thinly slice steak against the grain. For each sandwich: Spread 1 side of 1 bread slice with 1 Tbsp Pesto Mayonnaise. Top with 1 cup arugula, 2 slices tomato, 1/4 of the steak and another Tbsp Pesto Mayonnaise.

PREP: 8 min
GRILL: 12 min

SERVES 4

PER SERVING: 400 cal,
  25 g pro, 7 g car, 1 g fiber,
  30 g fat (8 g saturated fat),
  76 mg chol, 625 mg sod

TIP *Tubs of pesto may be found in the dairy or fresh pasta section of your market.*

PREP: 8 min
GRILL: 14 min

SERVES 4

PER SERVING: 325 cal,
  20 g pro, 9 g car, 3 g fiber,
  24 g fat (6 g saturated fat),
  52 mg chol, 498 mg sod

TIP To keep thin steaks and
  chops from curling, make a
  few 1/2-in.-deep cuts in the
  fat along the edges before
  cooking.

NOTE Never use a fork to flip
  vegetables and meat on the
  grill—juices will ooze out
  and food will become dry.
  Turn over with long-handled
  tongs, or cook food in an
  oiled, hinged grill basket.

Asian Grilled Beef Salad

VINAIGRETTE DRESSING
  3 Tbsp olive oil
  1 Tbsp red-wine vinegar
  1/4 tsp each salt and pepper
  1 Tbsp lime juice
  1/4 tsp hot-pepper sauce
  1/4 tsp sugar
One 12-oz boneless sirloin steak
1/2 tsp each salt and pepper
12-oz bag mixed green salad
2 kirby cucumbers, sliced
1/2 cup chopped mint
1/4 cup chopped unsalted peanuts

1 Heat barbecue grill.

2 Whisk Vinaigrette Dressing ingredients in a small bowl.

3 Sprinkle steak with salt and pepper, and grill 14 minutes (for medium-rare). Transfer to a cutting board; let stand for 15 minutes.

4 Dress salad; spread on serving platter. Top with cucumbers, mint and peanuts. Slice beef; add to platter.

Cuban Pork Sandwiches

1 tsp each ground cumin and dried oregano
1/4 tsp each salt and pepper
Four 1/4-in.-thick pork cutlets (about 12 oz)
1 medium onion, sliced
Garlic-flavor nonstick seasoning spray
4 Portuguese or kaiser rolls, split
8 thin slices each Swiss cheese and Virginia ham
1/2 cup sliced dill pickles

1 Heat barbecue grill. Mix the cumin, oregano, salt and pepper; sprinkle over both sides of the pork cutlets.

2 Coat the cutlets and onion slices with seasoning spray. Grill 3 minutes, turning cutlets and onions over once, until cutlets are cooked through and onions are slightly charred and crisp-tender.

3 Fill each roll with 2 slices *each* cheese and ham, 1 cutlet and 1/4 of the onions and pickles. Return to grill for 1 or 2 minutes to melt cheese, if desired.

PREP: 5 min
GRILL: 4 to 5 min

SERVES 4

PER SERVING: 507 cal, 39 g pro, 36 g car, 2 g fiber, 22 g fat (9 g saturated fat), 95 mg chol, 1,240 mg sod

NOTE *Stir pineapple chunks, chopped bell pepper and cilantro into deli coleslaw for a side dish that's good with these sandwiches.*

PREP: 10 min
GRILL: 24 to 29 min

SERVES 4

PER SERVING: 678 cal,
32 g pro, 96 g car, 9 g fiber,
19 g fat (6 g saturated fat),
65 mg chol, 1,053 mg sod

NOTE *If using bamboo or wooden skewers, soak them in water 20 to 30 minutes before grilling to keep them from burning.*

Spicy Pork Fajitas & Corn with Cumin Butter

8 fajita-size flavored or plain flour tortillas

SPICY BARBECUE SAUCE
1/2 cup bottled barbecue sauce
1/4 cup chopped fresh cilantro
2 tsp chopped, canned chipotle chiles in adobo sauce or 1 tsp hot-pepper sauce
2 tsp fresh lime juice

CUMIN BUTTER
1 1/2 Tbsp butter, softened
1 1/2 tsp fresh lime juice
1/4 tsp each salt, ground cumin and hot-pepper sauce
8 jalapeño peppers, halved lengthwise and seeded
One 12-oz whole pork tenderloin
2 large onions, cut crosswise in quarters
Nonstick cooking spray
4 ears fresh corn, husked
ACCOMPANIMENTS: lime wedges, fresh cilantro, shredded lettuce and halved avocados, seeded, to be eaten from skin with a spoon

1 Heat barbecue grill. Wrap tortillas in foil.

2 Mix ingredients for Spicy Barbecue Sauce and Cumin Butter in separate bowls.

3 Skewer peppers (see Tip and Note, *opposite and left*). Brush pork with 1/4 cup Spicy Barbecue Sauce. Coat the peppers and onions with nonstick spray.

4 Place pork, jalapeños and onions on grill. Grill peppers and onions, turning once, jalapeños 5 minutes, onions 12 minutes or until both are lightly charred and tender. Remove peppers from skewers. Place, with onions, on serving platter. Grill pork, turning to brown all sides, 17 to 20 minutes until an instant-read thermometer inserted in

center registers 155°F. Remove to a cutting board. Cover loosely with foil and let stand 8 to 10 minutes. (Temperature will rise about 5 degrees while pork stands.)

5 Place wrapped tortillas and corn on grill. Grill, turning both often, tortillas 5 minutes until warm, corn 7 to 9 minutes until lightly charred in a few places and kernels are tender when pierced. Spread or brush corn with Cumin Butter.

6 Thinly slice pork; add to platter and drizzle with remaining Spicy Barbecue Sauce. Let diners assemble their own fajitas. Serve with accompaniments.

TIP *Thread the peppers on side-by-side skewers to keep them from swiveling when turned. If you have a small grill basket, use that instead.*

Glazed Sausages & Onions with Corn

4 ears corn
1/4 cup honey mustard
2 Tbsp orange juice
1 Tbsp vegetable or light olive oil
4 fully cooked sausages (8 oz, see Tip)
8 oz reduced-fat kielbasa, cut in 4 pieces
2 medium red onions, sliced 1/2 in. thick
3 packed cups arugula or other salad greens

1 Heat barbecue grill. Pull corn husks back, but leave attached. Remove silks; place husks back up and wet ears under running water.

2 Put mustard, orange juice and oil in a small bowl; stir until blended. Brush some on the sausages and onions.

3 Grill sausages, onions and corn 10 to 12 minutes, turning sausages and corn often and onions once, until sausages are lightly charred and onions and corn are tender.

4 Arrange sausages on greens; top with onions and remaining mustard mixture. Serve with corn.

PREP: 10 minutes
GRILL: 10 to 12 minutes

SERVES 4

PER SERVING: 338 cal,
23 g pro, 39 g car, 6 g fiber,
11 g fat (3 g saturated fat),
65 mg chol, 1,125 mg sod

TIP You can use any fully cooked sausages.

GRILLING TIP

If you often struggle to get a charcoal fire going, go ahead and spend a little for a chimney starter. You'll wonder how you ever lived without it.

PREP:	25 min
COOK:	1 hr
GRILL:	12 to 14 min

SERVES 8

PER SERVING: 727 cal,
46 g pro, 29 g car, 1 g fiber,
47 g fat (17 g saturated fat),
187 mg chol, 1,134 mg sod

TIP *Boiling ribs before grilling gets rid of fat (which reduces fire flare-ups) and tenderizes the meat.*

PLANNING TIP *Can be prepared through Step 3 up to 2 days ahead.*

NOTE *To save the cooking water to use as a broth for soup, refrigerate until fat that rises to the top solidifies and can be lifted off. Refrigerate broth up to 2 days or freeze in airtight container(s) up to 3 months.*

Barbecue Ribs

2 whole racks pork spareribs (about 3 1/2 lb each)
2 onions, each cut in quarters
1 tsp each salt and pepper

BARBECUE SAUCE
1 bottle (20 oz) ketchup (2 cups)
1/3 cup firmly packed light-brown sugar
1/4 cup water
1 tsp freshly grated lemon peel
2 Tbsp lemon juice
4 cloves garlic, smashed
3/4 tsp ground ginger

1 Place spareribs (racks cut in half if necessary), onions, salt and pepper in a large pot with water to cover. (Or use 2 pots with half the onions, salt and pepper in each.) Bring to a boil, reduce heat, cover and simmer 1 hour or until meat on ribs is tender (see Tip).

2 Meanwhile bring Barbecue Sauce ingredients to boil in medium saucepan. Reduce heat; partially cover and simmer, stirring occasionally, 20 minutes to blend flavors. Let cool.

3 Remove ribs from pot (see Note). When cool enough to handle, place in 2 large, sturdy plastic ziptop bags. Add half the Sauce to each, press air from bags, seal and turn bags over a few times to coat ribs. Refrigerate up to 2 days.

4 Pour Sauce from bags into a bowl. Grill ribs 4 to 6 in. above heat source 12 to 14 minutes, basting a few times with the Sauce and turning ribs over occasionally to prevent burning. Discard remaining Sauce.

5 To serve, cut in 1-rib portions.

PREP: 8 min
GRILL: 11 to 13 min

SERVES 4

PER SERVING: 491 cal,
  29 g pro, 28 g car, 2 g fiber,
  28 g fat (9 g saturated fat),
  97 mg chol, 542 mg sod

TIP *Jars of jerk seasoning sauce may be found with the barbecue and hot pepper sauce in your supermarket.*

PREP: 10 min
GRILL: 16 to 18 min

SERVES 4

PER SERVING: 135 cal,
  2 g pro, 26 g car, 3 g fiber,
  4 g fat (0 g saturated fat),
  0 mg chol, 158 mg sod

Jerk-Seasoned Pork Burgers

1/4 cup light mayonnaise
2 Tbsp ketchup
2 tsp plus 2 Tbsp jerk seasoning sauce (see Tip, left)
4 hamburger buns
1 1/4 lb lean ground pork, shaped into four 4-in. patties
4 leaves green-leaf lettuce
1 large ripe tomato, cut in 8 slices

1 Heat barbecue grill or ridged grill pan. Combine mayonnaise, ketchup and 2 tsp jerk seasoning sauce in a small mixing bowl.

2 Grill buns, cut sides down, 1 minute or until browned. Remove to serving platter.

3 Spread 1 side of burgers with 1 Tbsp remaining jerk sauce. Place sauce side down on the grill; spread tops with the remaining sauce.

4 Grill burgers 5 to 6 minutes each side until an instant-read thermometer inserted from side of burgers to center registers 160°F.

5 Serve on buns with mayonnaise mixture, green-leaf lettuce and tomato slices.

GRILLED PINEAPPLE, PEPPERS & ONION

2 green bell peppers, quartered and seeded
Four 1-in.-thick slices fresh pineapple, pared (see Tip, right)
4 large 1/2-in.-thick slices Spanish onion
Nonstick cooking spray
1/4 cup bottled lowfat honey-Dijon dressing
GARNISH: chopped cilantro

1 Grill peppers 5 to 6 minutes per side until slightly charred and crisp-tender. Remove to serving platter.

2 Lightly coat pineapple and onion slices with nonstick

spray. Grill pineapple 2 minutes per side or until heated through and onion 3 minutes per side or until slightly charred and crisp-tender. Add to platter; drizzle with dressing and sprinkle with cilantro.

TIP *Pared and cored fresh pineapple can be found in the produce section of many supermarkets.*

Greek Butterflied Leg of Lamb

*1 boned, butterflied shank-half leg of lamb
(about 2 3/4 lb after boning), trimmed of visible fat*
1/2 cup bottled Greek vinaigrette dressing
GARNISH: *fresh rosemary sprigs*

1 Put lamb and vinaigrette in a 1-gal plastic ziptop food bag. Press out air, seal and refrigerate, turning bag occasionally, at least 8 hours or up to 24.

2 Heat barbecue grill over medium heat.

3 Remove meat from bag and place on grill. Discard bag with marinade.

4 Grill, turning lamb over once, 15 to 20 minutes on each side, until an instant-read thermometer inserted in thickest part of meat registers at least 140°F for medium-rare.

5 Transfer to cutting board and let stand 10 minutes (internal temperature will rise about 5 degrees while standing). Thinly slice meat, arrange on serving platter and garnish with rosemary sprigs.

PREP: 30 min plus
          at least 8 hr
          unattended
GRILL: 30 to 40 min

SERVES 6

PER SERVING: 321 cal,
44 g pro, 1 g car, 0 g fiber,
14 g fat (4 g saturated fat),
136 mg chol, 210 mg sod

MEDITERRANEAN COUSCOUS SALAD

Prepare **1 box (10 oz) plain couscous** as pkg directs; cool. Place in large bowl with **1 can (about 15 oz) chickpeas,** rinsed, **1 pt (12 oz) pear or grape tomatoes,** halved, **1 medium English seedless (hothouse) cucumber,** cut in chunks (2 1/2 cups), **1/2 cup thinly sliced red onion, 1/2 cup chopped fresh mint leaves, 1/3 cup pitted kalamata olives,** coarsely chopped, **1/3 cup bottled Greek vinaigrette** dressing. Toss to mix and coat.

Serves 6

PER SERVING: 261 cal,
8 g pro, 38 g car, 4 g fiber,
8 g 7 fat (4 g saturated fat),
0 mg chol, 275 mg sod

PREP: 5 min
BAKE: 1 1/2 hr
GRILL: 8 to 10 min

SERVES 4

PER SERVING: 846 cal,
52 g pro, 9 g car, 0 g fiber,
66 g fat (28 g saturated fat),
214 mg chol, 516 mg sod

SAUCY TIPS

- When making barbecue sauce, make an extra batch or two and freeze it in 1- or 2-cup containers.

- Don't put sweetened and oil-based sauces on food until it's almost finished grilling. Sweetened sauces tend to burn and oil has a tendency to drip and cause flare-ups.

Indian-Style Lamb Riblets

4 lb lamb riblets, trimmed of excess outer fat

SAUCE
1 1/2 cups plain nonfat yogurt
1 Tbsp grated fresh ginger
1 Tbsp curry powder
2 tsp minced garlic
1 tsp ground cumin
1/2 tsp each salt and ground red pepper (cayenne)

1 Heat oven to 350°F. Have ready a large roasting pan with rack. Pour 1/2 in. water into pan.

2 Place ribs on rack in pan. Cover with foil and bake 1 1/2 hours or until tender.

3 Meanwhile mix Sauce ingredients in a large bowl. Add hot ribs and toss until well coated.

4 Grill 4 to 6 in. from medium-hot (400°F) coals 8 to 10 minutes, turning a few times until browned.

Greek Grilled Swordfish and Vegetable Kabobs

MARINADE
- 1/2 tsp freshly grated lemon peel
- 2 Tbsp fresh lemon juice
- 2 Tbsp olive oil, preferably extra-virgin
- 1 Tbsp chopped flat-leaf (Italian) parsley leaves
- 1 Tbsp fresh oregano leaves or 1 tsp dried
- 1/2 tsp minced garlic
- 1/2 tsp salt
- 1/4 tsp freshly ground pepper
- 1 lb swordfish, cut in 1-in. cubes
- 2 medium-size yellow squash (about 6 oz each), cut in 12 chunks
- 12 large mushrooms, cut in half
- 4 scallions, cut in 1-in. pieces
- 12 cherry tomatoes

1 Have ready ten 18-in. or longer metal skewers (see Tip).

2 Mix Marinade ingredients in a small bowl. Spoon 2 Tbsp into medium-size bowl. Add swordfish and stir to coat. Let stand at room temperature 25 to 30 minutes.

3 Heat barbecue grill.

4 Meanwhile thread swordfish on 4 skewers, squash on 2 skewers, mushrooms and half the scallion pieces alternately on 2 more skewers and tomatoes and rest of scallions alternately on remaining 2 skewers. Brush the vegetables with remaining Marinade.

5 Grill fish and vegetables 4 to 6 in. from heat source, turning skewers occasionally, fish 6 minutes or until nearly opaque in center; vegetables 3 to 4 minutes until crisp-tender.

6 Remove fish and vegetables from skewers to a large platter or divide evenly among dinner plates.

PREP: 25 min
MARINATE: 25 to 30 min
GRILL: 6 min

SERVES 4

PER SERVING: 252 cal, 26 g pro, 11 g car, 3 g fiber, 12 g fat (2 g saturated fat), 44 mg chol, 402 mg sod

TIP If you don't have enough skewers, cook the vegetable kabobs first and remove from skewers (they'll taste fine at room temperature), then skewer and cook the fish.

NOTE Couscous makes a good side dish with grilled swordfish. This dried, fully cooked pasta is the size of tiny grains and needs only a 5-minute soak in hot water or broth and it's ready to serve. Look for couscous in the grain section of your supermarket.

PREP: 30 min
MARINATE: At least 2 hr
GRILL: 3 to 6 min

SERVES 4

PER SERVING: 423 cal,
  34 g pro, 22 g car, 4 g fiber,
  23 g fat (4 g saturated fat),
  142 mg chol, 1,081 mg sod

FYI *The marinade flavors the seafood and dresses the salad.*

Seafood Kabobs with Parmesan-Rosemary Toast and Arugula & Tomato Salad

MARINADE/DRESSING

  5 Tbsp olive oil

  1 Tbsp plus 1 tsp red-wine vinegar

  1 tsp minced garlic

  3/4 tsp salt

  1/2 tsp pepper

12 extra-large shrimp (about 12 oz), peeled and deveined

8 sea scallops (about 8 oz)

8 thin slices prosciutto (about 3 oz), cut in half lengthwise

Four 1/2-in.-thick slices from a small round loaf Italian or sourdough bread

1 Tbsp olive oil

ARUGULA & TOMATO SALAD

  2 large ripe tomatoes, (about 1 1/4 lb), cut in wedges, wedges cut in half

  1 bunch (about 4 oz) arugula, cut in bite-size pieces (about 4 loosely packed cups)

  1/2 cup sliced red onion

  1 Tbsp chopped fresh rosemary

  1 Tbsp grated Parmesan cheese

1 tsp chopped fresh rosemary

1 tsp grated Parmesan cheese

1 Have ready four 8-in. or longer skewers.

2 Put Marinade/Dressing ingredients in a small jar and shake to blend. Pour about 3 Tbsp into a gallon-size ziptop food bag. Close jar and refrigerate remaining mixture. Add shrimp and scallops to bag. Press out air, seal and turn to distribute Marinade. Refrigerate at least 2 hours or up to 8 hours, turning bag occasionally.

3 Thread shrimp and scallops alternately on skewers.

Discard Marinade in bag. Wrap 2 pieces prosciutto around seafood on each skewer. Brush both sides of bread with oil.

4 Heat barbecue grill. Lightly coat grill with nonstick cooking spray. Put Arugula & Tomato Salad ingredients in a large serving bowl. Toss to mix.

5 Cook bread and kabobs 4 to 6 in. from heat source, bread 1 to 2 minutes until bottom is lightly toasted. Turn slices over, sprinkle each slice with 1/4 tsp *each* rosemary and Parmesan. Grill bread 1 to 2 minutes longer until bottom is toasted, kabobs 1 1/2 to 3 minutes per side until shrimp and scallops are just barely opaque at center.

6 Add the reserved Marinade/Dressing to Salad. Toss to mix and coat.

"Just throw it on the grill!" It's a summertime anthem all right, but if you take it literally you'll probably end up with something charred on the outside and raw in the middle. That's where direct and indirect grilling come into play.

DIRECT HEAT *is best for quick-cooking foods such as frankfurters, hamburgers, cut-up chicken, steaks, chops, vegetables, kabobs and cut-up fish or shrimp.* **How To:** *Food is cooked on an uncovered grill, directly over light-gray ash-covered coals. The exception: Cook chicken parts (on the bone) with the grill cover closed. For gas grills, follow manufacturer's directions.*

INDIRECT HEAT *is best for foods that need longer cooking in less intense heat. Good candidates are whole chickens, Cornish hens, turkey, whole fish and pork or beef roasts.* **How To:** *Set a disposable foil pan under the food to be grilled. Build the fire to one side and place the food on the other, or build the fire around the pan in middle of the grill. For a gas grill, follow manufacturer's directions.*

Grilled Halibut Salad with Oranges

VINAIGRETTE DRESSING
   3 Tbsp olive oil
   1 Tbsp red-wine vinegar
   1/4 tsp each salt and pepper
2 navel oranges
Four 3/4-in.-thick halibut steaks (about 8 oz each)
1/2 tsp each salt and pepper
Nonstick cooking spray
5-oz bag baby spinach salad
1/3 cup sliced red onion
1/3 cup kalamata olives

1 Heat barbecue grill.
2 Prepare Vinaigrette Dressing in a small bowl.
3 Remove peel and white pith from navel oranges; cut into segments and squeeze juice from membranes into bowl with dressing.
4 Sprinkle halibut steaks with salt and pepper. Coat with nonstick cooking spray. Grill, turning over once, 8 minutes or until cooked through.
5 Add spinach salad, onion and olives to bowl with Dressing. Toss to coat. Serve halibut on salad.

PREP: 10 min
GRILL: 8 min

SERVES 4

PER SERVING: 383 cal,
   40 g pro, 15 g car, 4 g fiber,
   18 g fat (2 g saturated fat),
   59 mg chol, 802 mg sod

PREP: 35 min
GRILL: 6 min

SERVES 4

PER SERVING: 331 cal,
  21 g pro, 13 g car, 3 g fiber,
  23 g fat (3 g saturated fat),
  140 mg chol, 341 mg sod

GRILLING TIP

To keep small pieces of food from falling through the grates of the grill, use a wire grill basket or grill grid. Brush with oil to keep food from sticking.

Grilled Shrimp Salad

VINAIGRETTE DRESSING
  1/4 cup vegetable oil
  2 Tbsp extra-virgin olive oil
  2 Tbsp cider vinegar
  1 Tbsp minced shallot or white part of scallion
  1 tsp Dijon mustard
  1/4 tsp each salt and granulated sugar
1 lb medium-size shrimp (about 32), peeled and deveined
1 Tbsp chili powder
6 cups mixed salad greens (we used romaine, watercress,
  radicchio and arugula)
2 navel oranges, peeled, white pith removed, sectioned and
  cut in small pieces

1 Heat barbecue grill.

2 Shake all Vinaigrette Dressing ingredients in a small jar with tight-fitting lid. Pour about 3 Tbsp into a small bowl.

3 Have 4 long skewers ready. Thread about 8 shrimp per skewer. Brush with the 3 Tbsp Vinaigrette (discard any remaining in bowl), then sprinkle with the chili powder.

4 Grill shrimp 4 in. from heat source 3 minutes per side, or until just barely opaque.

5 Toss remaining Vinaigrette with greens and arrange on a large platter. Sprinkle with orange pieces and top with grilled shrimp, removed from skewers.

PREP: 6 min
COOK: 4 min
GRILL: 8 min

SERVES 4

PER SERVING: 338 cal,
  35 g pro, 1 g car, 0 g fiber,
  21 g fat (4 g saturated fat),
  69 mg chol, 448 mg sod

TIP *Grate the lemon peel before squeezing the lemon for juice.*

TOMATO-OLIVE PESTO SALAD

Coarsely chop **1/2 cup assorted pitted olives** in a food processor or with a large knife. Scrape into a small bowl, add **2 oz feta cheese,** crumbled and **1/4 cup chopped red onion** and toss to mix. Cover and refrigerate until ready to serve. To serve: Arrange **6 plum (Roma) tomatoes,** sliced on a serving platter. Top with olive mixture; sprinkle with **chopped parsley.**

SERVES 4

PER SERVING: 94 cal,
  3 g pro, 5 g car, 0 g fiber,
  7 g fat (0 g saturated fat),
  13 mg chol, 630 mg sod

Mediterranean Swordfish

LEMON-GARLIC AND MINT SAUCE
  1 1/2 tsp minced garlic
  3 Tbsp olive oil
  1/2 tsp freshly grated lemon peel (see Tip)
  2 Tbsp lemon juice
  1/4 tsp salt
  1/8 tsp pepper
1 Tbsp olive oil
1/4 tsp salt
1/8 tsp pepper
Four 3/4-in.-thick swordfish steaks (6 to 8 oz each)
2 Tbsp chopped fresh mint

1 LEMON-GARLIC AND MINT SAUCE: Heat garlic and 3 Tbsp olive oil in a medium skillet over medium heat 3 minutes or until garlic is translucent. Remove from heat and stir in remaining Sauce ingredients.

2 Heat barbecue grill.

3 Mix 1 Tbsp olive oil, 1/4 tsp salt and 1/8 tsp pepper in a small bowl. Brush on both sides of swordfish.

4 Place fish 4 to 6 in. from heat source. Grill, turning fish over once, until barely opaque when pierced in thickest part, about 8 minutes. Remove to a serving platter; gently pierce fish 3 or 4 times with a fork.

5 Meanwhile cook Sauce 1 minute longer or until hot. Stir in chopped mint and spoon over swordfish.

Salmon with Peach Salsa & Coleslaw

COLESLAW
   5 3/4 cups bagged coleslaw mix
   1/2 cup light mayonnaise
   1/3 cup finely chopped red onion
   2 Tbsp lime juice
   1 1/4 tsp sugar
4 pieces salmon fillet (about 5 oz each)
3 ripe peaches, halved and pitted
2 scallions, roots trimmed
Nonstick cooking spray
1/4 tsp salt

PEACH SALSA (see Tip)
   1/8 tsp salt
   1/3 cup finely chopped red bell pepper
   2 tsp lime juice
   1/4 to 1/2 tsp red pepper flakes, to taste

1 Heat barbecue grill.
2 Mix Coleslaw ingredients in a medium-size bowl. Cover and refrigerate.
3 Coat both sides of salmon, peach halves and scallions with nonstick spray. Sprinkle salmon with 1/4 tsp salt.
4 Grill salmon 3 to 5 minutes per side until barely opaque in center, peaches 8 minutes and scallions 2 minutes, turning both once, until slightly charred.
5 Dice peaches and slice scallions for Peach Salsa. Place in a bowl with rest of Salsa ingredients. Stir gently to mix.

PREP: 30 min
GRILL: 6 to 10 min

SERVES 4

PER SERVING: 492 cal,
   33 g pro, 32 g car, 3 g fiber,
   27 g fat (5 g saturated fat),
   94 mg chol, 586 mg sod

TIP Have Salsa ingredients, except grilled peaches and scallions, ready before you start grilling. Complete the salsa while the salmon finishes cooking.

PREP: 10 min
GRILL: 10 min

SERVES 4

PER SERVING: 410 cal,
  40 g pro, 9 g car, 1 g fiber,
  23 g fat (4 g saturated fat),
  118 mg chol, 263 mg sod

TIP *Have Salsa ingredients, except pineapple, ready in a bowl before you start cooking so, once grilled, pineapple can be diced and added while the salmon finishes cooking.*

Spicy Salmon with Pineapple Salsa

1 Tbsp curry powder
1/4 tsp ground red pepper (cayenne)
Four 3/4- to 1-in.-thick salmon steaks (about 8 oz each)
4 slices (about 1/2 in. thick), cored fresh or drained
  canned pineapple
Nonstick cooking spray

PINEAPPLE SALSA (see Tip)
  1/2 cup diced red bell pepper
  2 Tbsp sliced scallions
  1 tsp fresh lime or lemon juice
  1/4 tsp salt

1 Heat barbecue grill. Mix curry powder and ground red pepper, and sprinkle on both sides of salmon.

2 Coat salmon steaks and pineapple slices with nonstick cooking spray.

3 Grill pineapple and salmon 4 to 6 in. above heat source, turning both over once, 2 to 3 minutes for the pineapple, until lightly charred, and 10 minutes for the salmon or until just barely opaque at the center.

4 Dice pineapple, add to bowl with remaining Salsa ingredients and toss to mix. Serve with salmon.

Grilled Scampi Salad

1 lb medium shrimp (32 to 36), peeled and deveined

DRESSING
  1/2 cup bottled red-wine vinaigrette
  1 Tbsp each *Dijon mustard* and *minced garlic*
2 bags (10 oz each) *Italian- or European-blend salad greens*
1/2 cup *Parmesan fish-shaped crackers*
3 Tbsp *grated Parmesan cheese*

1 Heat barbecue grill. Prepare shrimp on skewers for grilling (see Tip).

2 Whisk Dressing ingredients in a salad bowl until blended. Remove 2 Tbsp and brush on shrimp. Add remaining ingredients to salad bowl.

3 Grill skewered shrimp 4 to 6 in. from heat source 4 to 5 minutes, turning once, until just barely opaque at center. Slide off skewers into salad bowl. Toss salad and serve.

PREP: 10 min
GRILL: 4 to 5 min

SERVES 4

PER SERVING: 268 cal, 23 g pro, 13 g car, 2 g fiber, 12 g fat (3 g saturated fat), 143 mg chol, 823 mg sod

TIP *Run 2 parallel skewers through the shrimp to keep them from swiveling when turned on the grill.*

TOMATO-OLIVE TOAST

TOPPING
  1 medium ripe tomato, *chopped*
  1 cup fresh basil leaves, *chopped*
  1/3 cup pitted ripe olives, *chopped*
  1/2 tsp *minced garlic*
1/2 a 1-lb loaf *Italian bread, cut in 3/4-in.-thick slices*

1 Mix Topping ingredients in a bowl.

2 Grill bread slices 4 to 6 in. from heat source 2 to 4 minutes, turning once until toasted. Spoon on Topping.

PREP: 5 min
GRILL: 2 to 4 min

SERVES 4

PER SERVING: 179 cal, 6 g pro, 32 g car, 3 g fiber, 3 g fat (1 g saturated fat), 0 mg chol, 432 mg sod

Creamy Red Pepper Dip

1 medium clove garlic, peeled
1 brick (8 oz) 1/3-less-fat cream cheese (Neufchâtel),
  softened
1 jar (7 oz) roasted red peppers, well drained
2 medium scallions, cut in short pieces
2 Tbsp fresh lemon juice
3/4 tsp ground cumin
ACCOMPANIMENTS: *fresh vegetables such as sliced cucumber,*
  blanched sugar snap peas, radishes and cherry tomatoes

Process garlic in a blender or food processor until finely chopped. Add remaining ingredients and process until smooth. Scrape into a serving bowl, cover and refrigerate until chilled or up to 3 days.

PREP: 5 min

MAKES 1 1/2 cups

PER 3 TBSP: 79 cal,
  3 g pro, 3 g car, 0 g fiber,
  6 g fat (4 g saturated fat),
  20 mg chol, 153 mg sod

PLANNING TIP *Can be made up to 3 days ahead.*

Grilled Corn and Black Bean Salsa

3 medium-size ears corn, husked
2 Anaheim chile peppers
1 can (16 oz) black beans, rinsed and drained
3 plum tomatoes, chopped
3 Tbsp fresh lemon juice
1/4 tsp each salt and pepper

Grill corn and chiles 8 minutes or until charred. Cut corn from cob (you should have about 1 1/2 cups). Peel peppers; remove and discard cores and seeds, then chop. Mix in a bowl with remaining ingredients.

Mango Salsa

1 cup each diced mango and cantaloupe
1 can (4 1/2 oz) chopped green chiles, drained
1/3 cup thinly sliced scallions
1/4 cup chopped cilantro
2 Tbsp fresh lime juice
Pinch ground red pepper (cayenne)

Combine all ingredients in a bowl. Serve immediately or refrigerate for up to 3 days.

Green Tomato Salsa

1 poblano chile pepper
1 cup finely chopped, seeded green tomatoes
1 jalapeño pepper, cored, seeded and minced
2 Tbsp chopped fresh cilantro
1/2 tsp ground cumin
2 Tbsp red-wine vinegar
1/4 cup diced red onion

Roast the poblano chile pepper. Peel, remove and discard core and seeds, then chop. Mix in a medium-size bowl with remaining ingredients.

Prep: 5 min

Makes 2 cups

Per 1/4 cup: 82 cal,
  3 g pro, 8 g car, 2 g fiber,
  5 g fat (1 g saturated fat),
  3 mg chol, 267 mg sod

FYI *The combination of peas and avocado tastes great, and using peas instead of a second avocado in this recipe saves about 30 g fat and more than 100 calories.*

Green Pea Guacamole

1 1/2 cups (10 oz) frozen green peas, thawed
1/2 cup loosely packed cilantro
1/4 cup reduced-fat sour cream
3 Tbsp fresh lemon juice
3/4 tsp salt
1/8 tsp hot-pepper sauce
1 ripe avocado, peeled, seeded and diced

Pulse all ingredients except avocado in a food processor until almost smooth. Gently stir in diced avocado.

Fresh Tomato Salsa

6 ripe plum tomatoes, seeded and diced
1/2 cup each chopped red onion and cilantro
2 Tbsp each minced jalapeño pepper, fresh lime juice,
  red-wine vinegar and olive oil
1 tsp minced garlic
ACCOMPANIMENTS: grilled flour tortillas, plain or flavored,
  cut in wedges

Mix all ingredients in a medium bowl. Let sit 30 minutes at room temperature for flavors to blend. Serve with Accompaniments.

PREP: 15 min plus 30 min unattended

MAKES 2 1/4 cups

PER 2 TBSP: 19 cal,
  0 g pro, 1 g car, 0 g fiber,
  2 g fat (0 g saturated fat),
  0 mg chol, 2 mg sod

PLANNING TIP *Refrigerate, tightly covered, up to 5 days.*

Layered Tex-Mex Dip

BEAN LAYER

　2 cans (16 oz each) *fat-free refried beans*
　2 Tbsp *lime juice*
　2 tsp *chili powder*
　1 tsp each *minced garlic, ground cumin and hot pepper sauce*

GUACAMOLE LAYER

　2 ripe *avocados*
　1 Tbsp each *fresh lime juice and chopped cilantro*
　1 tsp each *minced garlic and salt*
3/4 cup *reduced-fat sour cream*
2/3 cup *shredded Cheddar cheese*

SALSA LAYER

　1 large tomato, *seeded and chopped (1 cup)*
　1/4 cup *sliced scallions*
　1/4 cup *chopped cilantro*
　1 Tbsp *fresh lime juice*
　1/2 tsp *minced garlic*
　1/4 tsp *salt*
ACCOMPANIMENTS: *tortilla chips, lime wedges*

1 BEAN LAYER: Mix ingredients in a medium bowl. With rubber spatula, mound in center of a 12-in. or larger serving plate. Shape into a flat circle about 8 in. across.

2 GUACAMOLE LAYER: Halve avocados; scoop flesh into a medium bowl. Mash with lime juice, cilantro, garlic and salt until almost smooth. Spread on top of bean layer.

3 Top with sour cream, then sprinkle with cheese. Cover surface directly with plastic wrap to keep out air; refrigerate.

4 SALSA LAYER: Stir ingredients in a medium-size bowl. Cover and refrigerate.

5 Remove plastic wrap. Drain juices from Salsa; spoon over cheese. Surround Dip with chips and lime wedges, and serve extra chips in a basket.

PREP:　　30 min

SERVES 16

PER SERVING: 130 cal,
　6 g pro, 12 g car, 4 g fiber,
　7 g fat (2 g saturated fat),
　9 mg chol, 412 mg sod

PLANNING TIP *Prepare the lime juice, garlic and cilantro at the same time. May be assembled through Step 3 up to 1 day ahead. The Salsa may be made up to 8 hours before serving.*

PREP: 6 min

MAKES 1 3/4 cups

PER 2 TBSP: 22 cal,
 1 g pro, 3 g car, o g fiber,
 o g fat (o g saturated fat),
 2 mg chol, 27 mg sod

PREP: 7 min

MAKES 2 cups

PER 2 TBSP: 26 cal,
 1 g pro, 4 g car, o g fiber,
 o g fat (o g saturated fat),
 o mg chol, 89 mg sod

PREP: 5 min

MAKES 3 cups

PER 1/4 CUP: 35 cal,
 2 g pro, 6 g car, 1 g fiber,
 o g fat (o g saturated fat),
 o mg chol, 138 mg sod

Artichoke Dip

1/2 cup nonfat sour cream
3 Tbsp grated Parmesan cheese
2 scallions, cut in chunks
1 small clove garlic, chopped
1 can (14 oz) artichoke hearts, rinsed and drained

Process sour cream, Parmesan cheese, scallions and garlic in a food processor or blender until blended. Add artichokes and process just until finely chopped.

Chickpea and Red Pepper Dip

1 can (16 oz) chickpeas, rinsed and drained
1 jar (7 oz) roasted red peppers, rinsed and drained
1/2 cup plain nonfat yogurt
1 small clove garlic, chopped
1/4 tsp each salt and pepper

Process all ingredients in a food processor or blender until smooth.

Refried Bean Dip

1 can (16 oz) vegetarian refried beans
1 can (4.5 oz) chopped green chilies
1/2 tsp each ground cumin and garlic powder
1/4 cup chopped cilantro leaves

Mix all ingredients in a bowl until blended.

Corn and Black Bean Dip

1 can (15 oz) black beans, rinsed and drained
1 can (14 1/2 oz) salsa-style chunky tomatoes
1 can (7 oz) whole-kernel corn, drained
1 1/2 tsp hot chili powder
1/2 tsp salt

Process beans and tomatoes in a food processor or blender until finely chopped. Stir in remaining ingredients.

Creamy Spinach Dip

1 pkg (10 oz) frozen chopped spinach, thawed and squeezed dry
1 cup nonfat sour cream
2 scallions, cut in chunks
2 tsp dried dill weed
2 to 3 tsp lemon juice to taste
1/2 tsp salt

Process all ingredients in a food processor or blender until smooth.

PREP: 6 min

MAKES 2 CUPS

PER 2 TBSP: 29 cal,
 1 g pro, 6 g car, 1 g fiber,
 0 g fat (0 g saturated fat),
 0 mg chol, 248 mg sod

PREP: 8 min

MAKES 2 CUPS

PER 2 TBSP: 23 cal,
 2 g pro, 4 g car, 0 g fiber,
 0 g fat (0 g saturated fat),
 0 mg chol, 99 mg sod

Grilled Mushroom Napoleon

8 oz medium crimini mushrooms, briefly rinsed,
  trimmed and halved
8 oz medium shiitake mushrooms, stems removed, caps briefly
  rinsed and halved (see Tip)
1 large tomato, chopped
3 Tbsp chopped fresh flat-leaf parsley
1 Tbsp chopped fresh basil
3 Tbsp extra-virgin olive oil
1 Tbsp red-wine vinegar
1/2 tsp each salt and freshly ground pepper
Twelve 4 x 3 x 1/4-in. slices country bread
1/2 cup Asiago or Parmesan cheese shavings (removed from
  a chunk with a vegetable peeler)
GARNISH: basil sprigs

1 Heat grill to high. Set a vegetable grill basket or grill
grate on top; brush with oil.

2 Grill mushrooms 5 to 6 minutes or until browned and
tender. Transfer to a large bowl; add tomato, parsley, basil,
2 Tbsp of the oil, the vinegar, salt and pepper. Toss to mix.
Remove and reserve about 1/2 cup.

3 Grill bread 1 minute per side or until lightly toasted.
Brush with remaining 1 Tbsp oil.

4 Place 1 slice bread on each serving plate. Spoon half
the mushroom mixture, evenly divided, on the slices.
Sprinkle with some of the cheese shavings. Cover each
with another slice of bread, then the remaining mushroom
mixture and more cheese. Top with remaining bread,
reserved mushroom mixture and remaining cheese.
Garnish with basil; serve immediately.

PREP: 12 min
GRILL: 8 min

SERVES 4

PER SERVING: 288 cal,
  11 g pro, 23 g car, 3 g fiber,
  17 g fat (6 g saturated fat),
  13 mg chol, 676 mg sod

TIP *If shiitake mushrooms
are unavailable, substitute
button or additional crimini
mushrooms.*

GRILLING TIP

*A hinged vegetable grill basket
or grill grate makes it easier to
turn the mushrooms and keeps
them from falling into the coals.*

Grilled Vegetables

1 can (24 oz) white kidney beans, rinsed
1/2 cup packed fresh basil leaves, cut in narrow strips
1/2 cup bottled balsamic salad dressing
2 bell peppers, halved lengthwise
1 baby eggplant (about 5 oz), cut lengthwise in
    1/2-in.-thick slices
1 zucchini (about 10 oz), scrubbed, cut lengthwise in 6 slices
1 yellow summer squash (about 10 oz), scrubbed, cut
    lengthwise in 6 slices
1 small red onion, sliced in 1/2-in. rounds
4 plum tomatoes, halved lengthwise
Nonstick cooking spray
1 tsp each salt and pepper

1 Heat barbecue grill. Have a large platter ready.

2 Mix beans, basil and 1/4 cup of the balsamic dressing
in a medium bowl; stir to mix. Turn out onto serving platter.

3 Lightly coat vegetables with nonstick spray and season with salt and pepper.

4 Grill, turning once, eggplant and peppers 12 to 15
minutes (eggplant should be very tender and pepper skins
charred), squashes and onion 8 to 10 minutes until tender,
adding tomatoes for last 3 to 4 minutes.

5 Arrange vegetables on beans; drizzle with remaining
1/4 cup dressing.

PREP: 15 min
GRILL: 12 to 15 min

SERVES 4

PER SERVING: 298 cal,
  13 g pro, 41 g car, 11 g fiber,
  11 g fat (1 g saturated fat),
  0 mg chol, 1,014 mg sod

GRILLING TIPS

- Drizzle heads of garlic with olive oil. Wrap in foil and grill over indirect heat 40 minutes or until soft. Squeeze garlic from cloves onto grilled bread.

- Brush cut sides of Italian bread with olive oil. Grill 1 to 2 minutes until toasted and lightly charred. Serve, or cut in cubes to use as croutons.

SERVES 8

PER SERVING: 134 cal,
4 g pro, 20 g car, 5 g fiber,
6 g fat (0 g saturated fat),
0 mg chol, 97 mg sod

TIP The vinaigrette would
make a fine sauce to serve
over grilled fish, too.

GRILLING TIP

Grilled veggies and fish don't
need as much heat as thick
cuts of poultry or meat, so
don't overdo the briquettes.
You'll incinerate everything.

Grilled Summer Vegetables with Basil-Caper Vinaigrette

BASIL-CAPER VINAIGRETTE
1 cup loosely packed basil leaves, finely chopped
3 Tbsp olive oil, preferably extra-virgin
1 Tbsp red-wine vinegar
1 Tbsp bottled capers, drained
2 tsp Dijon mustard
1 tsp chopped fresh thyme leaves or 1/4 tsp dried
1/2 tsp minced garlic
Nonstick cooking spray
1 medium-size (1 1/4 lb) eggplant, cut crosswise in
1/2-in.-thick rounds
2 each medium-size red and yellow bell peppers, halved
lengthwise
2 each medium-size zucchini and yellow summer squash
(about 6 oz each), scrubbed and cut lengthwise in
1/4-in.-thick slices
1 large (1 lb) red onion, peeled and cut crosswise in
1/2-in.-thick slices
4 cups chopped ripe tomatoes
GARNISH: basil sprigs

1 Whisk all the Vinaigrette ingredients in a medium-size bowl until thoroughly blended.

2 Heat grill.

3 Lightly spray all vegetables except tomatoes with nonstick cooking spray. Grill sprayed vegetables 4 to 6 in. from heat source, turning vegetables over once: eggplant and peppers 12 to 15 minutes, squashes and onion 8 to 10 minutes, until all are tender (eggplant should be very tender) and slightly charred.

4 Arrange on serving platter with the tomatoes. Drizzle with Vinaigrette and garnish with basil.

TIP *Save the stems to slice and sauté to add to a gravy or a warm spinach salad, or fill an omelet.*

CLEANING MUSHROOMS

- *Just before using, wipe mushrooms with a damp cloth or a brush made for that purpose. (Available in cookware shops.)*

- *If mushrooms are very dirty, rinse quickly in cool water. Don't soak mushrooms since they absorb water like a sponge.*

Teriyaki-Grilled Portobello Mushrooms

2 Tbsp bottled teriyaki sauce
1 Tbsp vegetable oil
2 medium whole portobello mushrooms (about 14 oz), stems removed
1 tsp minced scallion
1/2 tsp shredded fresh ginger (optional)

1 Mix teriyaki sauce and vegetable oil. Brush on mushrooms until absorbed.

2 Grill 4 to 6 in. above hot coals 2 1/2 to 3 minutes per side until tender and lightly browned.

3 Cut mushroom caps in slices 1/4 to 1/2 in. wide. Sprinkle with scallion and ginger.

Pesto Portobello Burgers

4 large portobello mushrooms, stems twisted off (see Tip),
  caps cleaned
1 Tbsp olive oil
2 tsp reduced-sodium soy sauce

PESTO DRESSING
  1/4 cup light mayonnaise
  3 Tbsp reduced-fat basil pesto (see Note)
4 kaiser rolls or hamburger buns, split
4 lettuce leaves
4 large, thick slices tomato

1 Heat barbecue grill.

2 Brush mushroom caps all over with oil. Sprinkle undersides with soy sauce.

3 Grill 4 to 6 minutes, turning mushrooms once or twice, until dark brown, juicy and tender.

4 Meanwhile mix Pesto Dressing ingredients in a small bowl until well blended.

5 Line roll bottoms with lettuce. Top with mushrooms, sliced tomato, Dressing and roll tops.

PREP: 10 min
GRILL: 6 min

SERVES 4

PER SERVING: 336 cal,
  11 g pro, 42 g car, 4 g fiber,
  15 g fat (3 g saturated fat),
  8 mg chol, 642 mg sod

TIP Clean the mushroom stems, chop and freeze. Use to flavor soups, stews and pasta sauces.

NOTE Look for tubs of reduced-fat basil pesto in the dairy or fresh pasta section of your supermarket.

STORING MUSHROOMS

- Packaged mushrooms come in 4-, 8-, 10-, 12- and 16-oz containers. Store them in the original containers in the refrigerator.

- Store open packages or purchased loose mushrooms in paper bags. The porous bag allows mushrooms to breathe and stay fresh longer. Plastic bags cause rapid deterioration.

PREP: 20 min

SERVES 4

PER SERVING: 293 cal,
10 g pro, 33 g car, 3 g fiber,
14 g fat (5 g saturated fat),
25 mg chol, 1,018 mg sod

FYI *Ackawi, a popular Middle-Eastern cows' milk cheese that is now made in this country, is a salty brined cheese similar to feta.*

Middle-Eastern Bread Salad

MINT DRESSING
2 Tbsp olive oil, preferably extra-virgin
2 Tbsp fresh lemon juice
2 Tbsp chopped fresh mint leaves or 2 tsp dried
3/4 tsp minced garlic
3/4 tsp salt
1/4 tsp freshly ground pepper
3 pita, split, toasted and torn in 1-in. pieces
8 cups torn assorted salad greens (we used arugula, watercress and romaine)
3 plum tomatoes, cut in 1-in. chunks (1 cup)
1 small yellow pepper, halved lengthwise, cored, seeded and cut in strips
1/2 medium-size cucumber, peeled, seeded and cut in bite-size chunks
4 oz Ackawi (see FYI) or feta cheese, crumbled (1 cup)
1/4 cup chopped flat-leaf (Italian) parsley leaves

1 Whisk Dressing ingredients in a large serving bowl.

2 Add pita and the remaining ingredients. Toss to mix and coat. Serve immediately.

Grilled Panzanella

Four 3/4-in.-thick large slices country bread
2 yellow bell peppers
1 medium red onion, sliced 1/2 in. thick
3 large tomatoes, coarsely chopped
1 1/2 cups chopped English seedless (hothouse) cucumber
3 Tbsp capers
2 Tbsp extra-virgin olive oil
1 Tbsp red-wine vinegar, or more to taste
1 tsp salt
1/2 tsp freshly ground pepper

1 Heat grill to high and brush with oil. Grill bread 1 to 2 minutes per side or until lightly toasted. Set aside.

2 Grill peppers, turning several times, 10 minutes or until blackened on all sides. Place in a paper bag and let steam 10 minutes. When cool enough to handle, peel, core, seed and coarsely chop.

3 While grilled peppers cool, grill onion slices, turning them over once, 5 minutes or until nicely browned. When cool enough to handle, coarsely chop. Put onions and peppers in a large bowl.

4 Cut bread in 1/4-in. cubes and add to bowl along with the tomatoes, cucumber and remaining ingredients. Toss to mix. Let stand at room temperature about 30 minutes to allow flavors to develop.

5 Gently toss again just before serving.

PREP: 20 min
GRILL: 17 min
STAND: About 30 min

SERVES 6

PER SERVING: 143 cal,
 4 g pro, 21 g car, 3 g fiber,
 6 g fat (1 g saturated fat),
 0 mg chol, 709 mg sod

PEELING PEPPERS

- Place peppers 4 to 5 in. above hot coals. As they char, turn with tongs until completely blackened.

- When cool enough to handle, peel off easily removable charred skin with fingers. Do not rinse peppers.

Cold Peanut Noodle Salad

8 oz thin linguine pasta

DRESSING
- *2/3 cup bottled Thai-style peanut sauce*
- *2 Tbsp each cider vinegar and water*
- *1 tsp minced garlic*

1 lb Chinese cabbage, shredded (8 cups)
1/2 English seedless (hothouse) cucumber, quartered lengthwise and thinly sliced crosswise (2 cups)
2 medium carrots, shredded (1 1/2 cups)
1/3 cup each sliced scallions and chopped cilantro
1/4 cup chopped salted dry-roasted peanuts

1 Bring a large pot of lightly salted water to a boil. Add pasta and cook as package directs. Drain in a colander and cool under cold running water.

2 Meanwhile mix Dressing ingredients in a large serving bowl. Add cabbage, cucumber, carrots, scallions and cilantro; toss to mix. Add cooled pasta and toss to mix and coat. Sprinkle with peanuts.

PREP AND COOK: 20 min

SERVES 6

PER SERVING: 289 cal,
10 g pro, 44 g car, 6 g fiber,
8 g fat (1 g saturated fat),
0 mg chol, 499 mg sod

SERVES 4 as a main dish,
       8 as a side dish

PER SERVING without stuffed
  grape leaves (for 4): 348 cal,
  11 g pro, 16 g car, 4 g fiber,
  27 g fat (10 g saturated fat),
  50 mg chol, 1,212 mg sod

Greek Salad

1 bag (10 oz) hearts of romaine salad blend (8 cups)
1 pkg (8 oz) feta cheese (any flavor), cut or broken in chunks
1 can (10 oz) stuffed grape leaves (optional)
12 good-quality oil-cured olives, such as kalamata
12 slices English seedless (hothouse) cucumber
1 cup matchstick-cut carrots
4 thin slices red onion
4 bell pepper rings
1 large ripe tomato, cut in wedges
1/2 cup bottled Greek or red-wine vinaigrette
ACCOMPANIMENT: *warmed pita*

Place salad blend in a large bowl or on a large serving platter. Top with cheese, grape leaves, olives and vegetables; drizzle with vinaigrette. Serve with pita.

STOCK YOUR MEDITERRANEAN PANTRY
with these and you'll have the basics for zillions of delicious dishes:

- *olive oil*
- *red-wine vinegar*
- *dried or fresh herbs and spices, especially basil, cilantro, parsley, thyme, oregano, cumin, mint, hot pepper and black pepper*
- *garlic*
- *olives*
- *capers*
- *sundried tomatoes*
- *pine nuts and walnuts*
- *raisins and other dried fruit*
- *plain yogurt*

- *rice, pasta (including couscous), bulgur and other grains*
- *pita bread, Italian and French bread*
- *mozzarella and feta cheese*
- *sesame seeds, or sesame paste or oil*
- *canned or dried chickpeas, lentils and other varieties of beans*
- *fresh vegetables, especially onions, tomatoes, bell peppers and eggplant*
- *fresh fruit, particularly lemons and other citrus varieties*

Spinach Salad with Tofu-Sesame Dressing

1 block (12 oz) soft tofu, chilled, drained, excess moisture pressed out gently with paper towels
1/2 cup bottled Oriental dressing
1 bag (10 oz) fresh spinach
3/4 cup thinly sliced red radishes
1 pkg (8 oz) sliced mushrooms
4 strips bacon, cooked crisp, drained and crumbled
2 Tbsp toasted sesame seeds (see Tip)

1 Cut half the block of tofu into large cubes, place in a small bowl and reserve.

2 Purée rest of tofu and Oriental dressing in food processor or blender until smooth.

3 Toss spinach, radishes, mushrooms and bacon in a large serving bowl to mix. Top with reserved tofu and sesame seeds. Serve with dressing.

PREP: 15 min

SERVES 4

PER SERVING: 211 cal,
  10 g pro, 14 g car, 4 g fiber,
  13 g fat (2 g saturated fat),
  5 mg chol, 605 mg sod

TIP To toast sesame seeds, stir in a small skillet over medium heat until golden brown.

PER 1-CUP SERVING: 47 cal,
1 g pro, 12 g car, 2 g fiber,
0 g fat (0 g saturated fat),
0 mg chol, 308 mg sod

TIP To seed the cucumber, cut
it in half lengthwise, then
scrape out seeds by running
the tip of a teaspoon down
its length.

PLANNING TIP Can be made
up to 1 day ahead.

Firecracker Coleslaw

DRESSING
 1/4 cup distilled white vinegar
 1 tsp grated lime peel
 3 Tbsp fresh lime juice
 2 Tbsp honey
 1 tsp salt
 1/2 tsp crushed red pepper
1/2 small head green cabbage
3 small carrots
1 medium cucumber, seeded (see Tip)
1 medium red bell pepper, seeded, cut in sixths
1/2 small red onion

1 Whisk Dressing ingredients in large bowl until blended.

2 Using slicing disk of food processor or a long, sharp knife, thinly slice the cabbage (you should have 4 packed cups), carrots, cucumber, red pepper and onion. Add to Dressing; toss to mix and coat. Cover and refrigerate at least 2 hours for flavors to blend.

3 Drain juices from bottom of bowl. Transfer coleslaw to a medium serving bowl.

Carolina Black-Eyed Pea Salad

DRESSING

2 Tbsp each *extra-virgin olive oil and red-wine vinegar*
2 tsp *Dijon mustard*
1 tsp each *salt and pepper*
2 cans (15 1/2 oz each) *black-eyed peas, rinsed*
3 *ripe tomatoes, cut in chunks*
1/2 cup *thinly sliced red onion*
1 bag (10 oz) *washed spinach, tough stems discarded,
  leaves chopped*
4 *strips bacon, cooked crisp, then crumbled*
1/2 cup *toasted pecans, coarsely chopped (see Tip)*

1 Whisk Dressing ingredients in large serving bowl. Stir in peas, tomatoes and onion. Cover and refrigerate.

2 Just before serving: Add spinach; toss to mix. Sprinkle with bacon and pecans.

PREP: 10 min

SERVES 8

PER SERVING: 200 cal,
  8 g pro, 20 g car, 2 g fiber,
  10 g fat (2 g saturated fat),
  3 mg chol, 726 mg sod

TIP *To toast pecans, cook in a nonstick skillet over medium-low heat, stirring often, 5 to 6 minutes.*

PLANNING TIP *The nuts can be toasted up to 1 week ahead, the spinach and bacon prepared up to 1 day ahead. Refrigerate separately. Prepare the salad through Step 1 up to 8 hours before serving.*

PREP: 20 min
COOK: 10 min

MAKES 11 cups

PER 1/2 CUP: 121 cal, 3 g pro,
19 g car, 1 g fiber, 4 g fat
(1 g saturated fat), 0 mg chol,
132 mg sod

TIP English cucumbers aren't
waxed, so they don't need
peeling. You can substitute 2
regular cucumbers, but peel
or scrub them to remove
wax coating.

PLANNING TIP Prepare up to 2
days ahead. Bring to room
temperature before serving.

Summer Pasta Salad

1 box (1 lb) orzo (rice-shaped pasta)
1 1/2 lb tomatoes (3 large), coarsely chopped
1 long English seedless (hothouse) cucumber, cut in bite-size
  pieces (see Tip)
1 bunch scallions, thinly sliced

DRESSING
  1 1/2 cups bottled spicy-hot 8-vegetable juice
  2 tsp freshly grated lemon peel
  1/3 cup each fresh lemon juice and olive oil, preferably
    extra-virgin
  1 Tbsp minced garlic
  3/4 tsp each salt and pepper, preferably freshly ground

1 Cook orzo as directed on box. Drain well. Place in a
large bowl and add Dressing ingredients while still warm.

2 Add remaining ingredients and toss gently to mix.
Cover and refrigerate.

Watermelon & Nectarines in Lime Syrup

1/3 cup sugar
3 Tbsp water
2 Tbsp fresh lime juice (see Tip)
6 cups cubed seedless or seeded watermelon
3 ripe nectarines
1 tsp freshly grated lime peel

1 Combine sugar and water in a small saucepan. Bring to a boil; reduce heat and simmer until sugar dissolves. Remove from heat; stir in lime juice. Refrigerate until cold. Refrigerate watermelon in serving bowl.

2 Shortly before serving: Cut nectarines in wedges; add to watermelon. Stir lime peel into syrup and drizzle over fruit; toss to mix and coat.

Watermelon Dessert Salsa

2 cups finely diced watermelon
1 navel orange, diced
1 cup strawberries, coarsely chopped
1 to 2 Tbsp lemon juice
1 Tbsp honey
1/8 tsp ground red pepper (cayenne)
ACCOMPANIMENT: frozen lowfat yogurt or fruit sorbet and biscotti

Mix all ingredients in a medium-size bowl. Refrigerate at least 1 hour before serving.

PREP: 20 min
CHILL: About 1 hr

SERVES 8

PER SERVING: 96 cal, 1 g pro, 23 g car, 1 g fiber, 1 g fat (0 g saturated fat), 0 mg chol, 3 mg sod

TIP *Grate the peel before juicing the lime.*

PLANNING TIP *Can be prepared through Step 1 up to 4 hours ahead.*

PREP: 15 min
CHILL: At least 1 hr

MAKES 3 CUPS

PER 3-OZ SERVING: 35 cal, 1 g pro, 9 g car, 1 g fiber, 0 g fat (0 g saturated fat), 16 mg chol, 2 mg sod

FYI *This recipe is photographed page 75 (far right).*

PREP: 20 min
FREEZE: About 4 hr

SERVES 10

PER SERVING: 84 cal,
  1 g pro, 21 g car, 1 g fiber,
  0 g fat (0 g saturated fat),
  0 mg chol, 2 mg sod

FYI *Granita, unlike ice cream or sherbet, isn't smooth, but has coarse, frozen crystals. You'll need a food processor to make this version.*

PLANNING TIP *The granita freezes well up to 1 week.*

Watermelon-Grapefruit Granita

2 medium grapefruit, preferably pink or red
6 cups watermelon chunks (from a 5-lb watermelon), seeded
1/2 cup sugar
GARNISH: *small watermelon wedges, grapefruit sections and mint sprigs*

1 Have ready a 9-in. square metal pan.

2 Scrub grapefruit under cold running water. Finely grate 1 Tbsp peel from 1 grapefruit; set peel aside. With a sharp knife, cut peel and white pith from both grapefruit. Holding grapefruit over a bowl, cut between membranes to release sections. Squeeze juice from membranes into bowl.

3 Put grapefruit sections, juice, grated peel, watermelon and sugar into a food processor (in 2 batches if necessary). Pulse until liquefied. Pour into metal pan.

4 Place pan in freezer. When mixture starts to freeze, use a rubber spatula to fold frozen sides into center of pan. Repeat every 30 minutes for about 4 hours until mixture is completely frozen. Serve or cover pan tightly with foil and freeze up to 1 week.

5 Scrape surface of granita with a sturdy metal spoon (or ice cream spade or scoop) and place in serving dishes. Garnish with melon, grapefruit and mint.

Layered Fruit Salad

1/2 large pineapple, peeled and cored
1 1/4-lb wedge watermelon, preferably seedless
1/2 large cantaloupe, seeds removed
3 kiwi, peeled
1 pt (12 oz) strawberries, hulled and rinsed
1 cup seedless red grapes

1 Have ready a wide-mouth 3-qt container, preferably clear glass or plastic, or a deep 3-qt bowl.

2 Cut pineapple, watermelon, cantaloupe and kiwi in bite-size chunks; halve strawberries.

3 Layer fruits attractively in container. Cover and refrigerate until ready to serve.

PREP: 35 min

SERVES 8

PER SERVING: 111 cal,
  2 g pro, 27 g car, 4 g fiber,
  1 g fat (0 g saturated fat),
  0 mg chol, 8 mg sod

TIP *You can vary fruits based on preference or availability.*

PLANNING TIP *Can be prepared up to 1 day ahead.*

PREP: 30 min

SERVES 6

PER SERVING: 215 cal,
  2 g pro, 55 g car, 5 g fiber,
  1 g fat (0 g saturated fat),
  0 mg chol, 7 mg sod

TIP *The slightly peppery seeds of a papaya are edible. If you like them, sprinkle them over the fruit.*

Island Ambrosia

GINGER SYRUP
  1/4 cup each sugar and water
  1 Tbsp grated fresh ginger
1 ripe medium pineapple, leaves and skin cut off;
  pineapple quartered lengthwise
1 ripe medium papaya, peeled, quartered lengthwise;
  seeds scooped out
2 ripe mangoes, peeled, fruit cut from seed
4 ripe kiwi, peeled, halved lengthwise
GARNISH: sweetened, shredded coconut, toasted as pkg directs

1 Mix ingredients for Ginger Syrup in a small bowl. Leave at room temperature while preparing fruits.

2 Cut woody core from pineapple and discard. Cut pineapple in chunks; place in a large bowl.

3 Cut papaya and mangoes in chunks. Add to bowl. Thinly slice kiwi crosswise; add to bowl.

4 Pour Ginger Syrup through a small, fine sieve over bowl of fruit. Stir fruit gently with a rubber spatula to coat. Serve or cover and refrigerate up to 8 hours. Bring to room temperature to serve. Garnish with toasted coconut.

Grilled Apples

8 large cooking apples such as Granny Smith,
*   Royal Gala, Jonathan or Braeburn*
4 long metal skewers
4 Tbsp butter or margarine, melted
1/2 cup honey
ACCOMPANIMENT: *vanilla or cinnamon ice cream*

PREP: 8 min
GRILL: 15 to 20 min

SERVES 8

PER SERVING: 217 cal,
   0 g pro, 44 g car, 4 g fiber,
   6 g fat (4 g saturated fat),
   16 mg chol, 59 mg sod

1 Rinse and dry apples. Remove stems, but leave apples whole and don't remove cores.

2 Using a citrus-peel stripper or vegetable peeler, decoratively remove 6 narrow strips of peel from top to bottom of each apple.

3 Thread 2 apples on each skewer. Brush them lightly with some of the butter.

4 Grill 4 to 6 in. above medium-hot coals 15 to 20 minutes, turning skewers occasionally, until apples are slightly softened.

5 Remove from grill, brush with remaining butter, then the honey. Serve hot.

PREP: 10 min

SERVES 2 (1 to 1 1/2 cups each)

PER SERVING: 108 cal,
5 g pro, 19 g car, 1 g fiber,
2 g fat (1 g saturated fat),
6 mg chol, 71 mg sod

PER SERVING: 117 cal,
6 g pro, 19 g car, 2 g fiber,
2 g fat (1 g saturated fat),
6 mg chol, 80 mg sod

PER SERVING: 153 cal,
6 g pro, 31 g car, 5 g fiber,
2 g fat (1 g saturated fat),
5 mg chol, 62 mg sod

PER SERVING: 207 cal,
6 g pro, 44 g car, 4 g fiber,
2 g fat (1 g saturated fat),
5 mg chol, 72 mg sod

SUPER SMOOTHIES

BASIC DIRECTIONS

For the freshest flavor, use ripe fruit (the riper the fruit, the sweeter the smoothie). In fact, smoothies are a great way to use overripe or bruised fruit.

Choose your favorite smoothie, then process the fruit, liquid and flavoring in a blender (for silkiest texture), in a food processor or with an immersion blender until smooth. Add some sweetener if desired.

Tropical Fling

1/2 cup each ripe pineapple and mango, cut up
1/2 cup each plain lowfat yogurt and 1% lowfat milk
2 tsp fresh lime juice

Purple Pleasure

1/2 pt (generous 1 cup) blueberries
3/4 cup plain lowfat yogurt
1/4 cup 1% lowfat milk
3/4 tsp vanilla extract

Berry Delicious

1 pt (12 oz) strawberries, hulled and cut up
1 ripe banana, cut up
1/2 cup plain lowfat yogurt
1/3 cup 1% lowfat milk

Summer Sweet

3 medium (1 lb) ripe nectarines, cut up
1/2 cup plain lowfat yogurt
1/3 cup 1% lowfat milk
2 Tbsp minced crystallized ginger

MARGARITAS

- *Margaritas, or "little daisies," are a fine accompaniment to spicy food.*

BASIC DIRECTIONS

Chill 4 glasses in the freezer. Whirl crushed ice and the remaining ingredients, except garnish, in a blender until frothy and slushy. Pour into glasses, garnish and serve immediately.

Classic

You'll need four 8-oz glasses

- *If desired, wet rim of each glass with a lime wedge, then dip rim in kosher salt to coat.*

3 cups coarsely crushed ice
2/3 cup tequila
1/2 cup Triple Sec (orange-flavored liqueur)
1/2 cup fresh lime juice
3 Tbsp superfine sugar
GARNISH: *lime slices*

Pineapple

You'll need four 12- to 14-oz glasses

- *Start with the smaller amount of sugar, then taste and add more if you like.*

2 1/2 cups coarsely crushed ice
1 3/4 cups chilled pineapple juice
1/3 cup tequila
1/2 cup Triple Sec (orange-flavored liqueur)
1/3 cup fresh lime juice
1 or 2 Tbsp superfine sugar
GARNISH: *pineapple spears*

SERVES 4

PER SERVING: 226 cal,
0 g pro, 21 g car, 0 g fiber,
0 g fat (0 g saturated fat),
0 mg chol, 0 mg sod

SERVES 4

PER SERVING: 212 cal,
1 g pro, 29 g car, 0 g fiber,
0 g fat (0 g saturated fat),
0 mg chol, 1 mg sod

Strawberry

You'll need four 10-oz glasses

2 1/2 cups coarsely crushed ice
2 cups sliced ripe strawberries
1/2 cup tequila
1/2 cup Triple Sec (orange-flavored liqueur)
1/2 cup plus 2 Tbsp fresh lime juice
1/4 cup superfine sugar
GARNISH: whole strawberries

White Wine Margaritas

· *This new twist on the margarita is a refreshing wine cooler.*

You'll need four 12- to 14-oz glasses

2 cups coarsely crushed ice
2 cups chilled dry white wine
3/4 cup Triple Sec (orange-flavored liqueur)
1/4 cup plus 2 Tbsp fresh lime juice
3 Tbsp superfine sugar
GARNISH: mint sprigs

SERVES 4

PER SERVING: 238 cal,
 1 g pro, 30 g car, 2 g fiber,
 0 g fat (0 g saturated fat),
 0 mg chol, 1 mg sod

SERVES 4

PER SERVING: 247 cal,
 0 g pro, 26 g car, 0 g fiber,
 0 g fat (0 g saturated fat),
 0 mg chol, 6 mg sod

PREP: 20 min
COOK: 5 min

SERVES 8

PER SERVING: 209 cal,
  0 g pro, 55 g car, 0 g fiber,
  0 g fat (0 g saturated fat),
  0 mg chol, 1 mg sod

TIP *Before juicing, wash and dry 4 of the lemons, then use a vegetable peeler to peel long strips from them.*

PLANNING TIP *Can be made up to 1 week ahead.*

Thirst-Quenchin' Lemonade

6 cups water
2 cups sugar
Peel from 4 lemons (see Tip)
2 cups fresh lemon juice (about 9 large lemons)
GARNISH: *mint sprigs, lemon slices*

1 Boil 2 cups water, the sugar and lemon peel in a medium saucepan 5 minutes.

2 Discard peel. Cool, pour into a large pitcher and stir in the lemon juice and remaining 4 cups water. Cover and refrigerate.

3 Serve in tall ice-filled glasses garnished with the mint sprigs and lemon slices.

Rainbow Punch

1 1/2 cups each *orange juice and pineapple juice*
1/4 cup *fresh lime juice*
1 tsp *grenadine syrup (see Box, right)*
1/2 tsp *bitters (see Box, right)*
1 cup *club soda*
GARNISH: *maraschino cherries and orange slices*

1 Mix orange, pineapple and lime juices, grenadine and bitters in a glass measure or pitcher.

2 Pour into 4 ice-filled tall glasses. Top each with 1/4 cup soda. Garnish with cherries and orange slices.

Lemon Daisy

1/2 cup *grenadine syrup (see Box, right)*
1/3 cup *fresh lemon juice*
2 cups *club soda*
2 cups *lemon-flavored soda*
GARNISH: *lemon peel*

1 Mix grenadine and lemon juice in a glass measure.

2 Pour into ice-filled wine goblets. Top each with 1/2 cup of each soda. Garnish with peel.

PREP: 5 min

SERVES 4

PER SERVING: 105 cal,
  1 g pro, 26 g car, 0 g fiber,
  0 g fat (0 g saturated fat),
  0 mg chol, 14 mg sod

PREP: 5 min

SERVES 4

PER SERVING: 120 cal,
  0 g pro, 31 g car, 0 g fiber,
  0 g fat (0 g saturated fat),
  0 mg chol, 39 mg sod

BITTERS AND GRENADINE

- *Bitters is a liquid used to flavor drinks and foods and as a digestive aid. A readily available brand is Angostura.*

- *Grenadine, a sweet, red syrup, is used to add color and flavor to drinks and desserts. Some brands contain alcohol; check the label.*

- *Look for both in your supermarket's cocktail-mix section.*

PREP: 8 min
STEEP & STAND: 6 min

MAKES 16 CUPS

PER 1-CUP SERVING: 87 cal,
  0 g pro, 22 g car, 0 g fiber,
  0 g fat (0 g saturated fat),
  0 mg chol, 5 mg sod

Lemon-Raspberry Iced Tea

16 cups water
10 tea bags
1 1/2 cups sugar
1 bag (12 oz) frozen unsweetened raspberries
1/4 cup fresh lemon juice

1 Bring water to a boil in a 5- to 6-quart pot. Remove pot from heat and add all the tea bags. Let steep 3 minutes, then remove bags.

2 Add remaining ingredients and let stand 2 to 3 minutes, stirring occasionally, until raspberries have thawed.

3 Pour tea through a fine strainer into a large pot or bowl (not aluminum) or a few large pitchers. Discard berries. Store at room temperature up to 1 day or refrigerate up to 4 days. Serve over ice.

Strawberry-Lemon Punch

1 can (12 oz) frozen pink lemonade concentrate
1 pint (12 oz) ripe strawberries, reserve 8 with tops for garnish,
  rinse and hull the rest (2 cups)
6 1/4 cups cold water
1 quart ginger ale
GARNISH: whole strawberries

1 Process lemonade concentrate, hulled strawberries and 1 cup of the water in blender or food processor until berries are liquefied.

2 Pour lemonade mixture into a pitcher or punch bowl. Stir in remaining 5 1/4 cups cold water. Gradually stir in ginger ale. Serve over ice. Garnish with berries.

PREP: 10 min

MAKES 12 CUPS

PER 12-OZ SERVING: 153 cal, 0 g pro, 39 g car, 1 g fiber, 0 g fat (0 g saturated fat), 0 mg chol, 11 mg sod

PLANNING TIP *Can be prepared through Step 1 up to 8 hours ahead and refrigerated.*

Index of Ingredients

Photo credits

Cover: Charles Schiller; pp. 8, 11, 12: John Uher; p. 15: Charles Schiller; p. 16: John Uher; pp. 19, 20, 23: Charles Schiller; p. 24: Ann Stratton; pp. 26, 29, 30, 33: Charles Schiller; p. 34: Mark Thomas; p. 37: John Uher; p. 38: Jacqueline Hopkins; p. 41: Charles Schiller; pp. 42, 45, 46: John Uher; pp. 49, 51, 52: Charles Schiller; pp. 55, 56: John Uher; pp. 59, 60: Charles Schiller; p. 63: Mark Needham; p. 66: John Uher; p. 69: Jacqueline Hopkins; p. 70: Mark Thomas; p. 72: Charles Schiller; p. 75: John Uher; p. 76: Charles Schiller; p. 77: Jacqueline Hopkins; p. 78: Charles Schiller; p. 82: Ann Stratton; p. 84: Charles Schiller; p. 87: John Uher; p. 88: Christina Lessa; pp. 89, 91: Charles Schiller; p. 92: Ann Stratton; pp. 94, 97, 98: Jacqueline Hopkins; pp. 101, 102: Charles Schiller; p. 105: Mark Thomas; p. 106: Jacqueline Hopkins; p. 109: John Uher; p. 110: Charles Schiller; p. 113: John Uher; p. 114: Lisa Koenig; pp. 117, 119: John Uher; p. 120: Charles Schiller; p. 122: Charles Schiller; p. 123: Mark Needham; back cover, clockwise from top left: Charles Schiller; Jacqueline Hopkins; Charles Schiller.

Acknowledgments

The publisher wishes to thank Jane Chesnutt; Ellen R. Greene, Nancy dell'Aria, Mary Ellen Banashek, Marisol Vera, Sue Kakstys, Michele Fedele, Robb Riedel, Kim Walker, Greg Robertson, Margaret T. Farley; Cathy Dorsey; and all the photographers whose images are reproduced in the book.